Woolgar River Curse

Receiving a phone call announcing that you are the heir to a 70,000 acre cattle property complete with a five-bedroom mansion would be like winning the Lotto.

But to Gus and Lynette Teague, it was the beginning of a discovery into corruption, deceit, tragedy and murder.

Was it really an 'Aboriginal Curse' on that property that caused the death of a family of five, or simply tragic events

Other books by Max Barrington

Task:
I was looking to make a few dollars until my next work project started. "Check out the Air Tasking pages on Facebook," they said.
An Australian road trip from Cairns to Darwin turns into Mystery, Intrigue and Life Threatening Danger

Dying to Find Gold:
Fossicking for Gold in Australia is a popular activity
But when Mick West's, best mate goes missing whilst on a fossicking trip
The police suspect Mick of murder

Harry Croft:
When Harry's beloved wife is taken from him by reckless youths in a stolen car, he decides to reinstate justice the way it was when he was a police sergeant many years before

The New March:
It was a hot day in the Far Northern Coastal Australian Town
The first thing that Mitchell wanted as he walked into the sleepy towns public bar was a cool drink.
The last thing that Mitchell wanted was an altercation with an Australian Aboriginal that would result in the death of five people.

Dedicated to the Love of my Life
"Lynette"

Table of Contents

The Call — *11*
Mrs Sonia Teague — *24*
Woolgar River Park — *32*
Who is Barry — *72*
The Curse — *91*
Lachlan Teague — *105*
The Agistment Stock — *126*
A Case For Murder — *136*
Owen Harrigan — *156*

Max Barrington

This book is a work of fiction. Unless otherwise indicated, all the names, characters, businesses, places, events and incidents in this book are either the product of the author's imagination or used in a fictitious manner. Any resemblance to actual persons, living or dead, or actual events is purely coincidental.

The Call

The mobile phone was playing the ringtone of the James Bond opening theme, and it kept going, and going, then stopped, then restarted, then stopped, then restarted, "Hello, this is Gus" said the sleepy voice. "Good morning, is that Angus Teague," asked the voice.
"It is, and who is calling" a sleepy, but starting to awaken Gus, replied.
"My name is Malcolm Davies, Mr Teague. I'm a solicitor at Wedderburn & Holt, could you please tell me your date of birth, Mr Teague".
"Well, Mr Davies, is it? If you can tell me what it is that you have contacted me about, then I may talk to you, but, you had better be quick because I'm about to hang up", said Gus.

"Please, please don't hang up Mr Teague, it's about your Uncle, Lachlan Teague"
"Is he sick?" asked Gus, trying to think of who Lachlan is.
" He died Mr Teague, he died some time ago, it has taken some time for us to locate you".

Gus's mind was trying hard to remember his Uncle Lachlan. Yes, yes, Dad's younger brother that nobody hears from!

"Oh, I, I wasn't aware, I haven't seen him since I was a kid in Scotland" responded Gus, "last time I heard, I think it was when he bought a property near Richmond in Queensland, I think,…it was ten years before my father died, hmmm, that's about sixteen years ago".

"Well straight to the point, Mr Teague, you are the sole beneficiary of his estate, according to his will", explained Malcolm Davies.

Angus Teague, was born in Canonbie, Scotland. The only son of Alisdair and Eileen. He came to Australia with his parents in 1950 as a migrant. They stayed at the transitional hostel near Sydney, New South Wales, for a short period of time, before moving to Yass also in New South Wales,
where Alisdair Teague took up an established Romney sheep breeding property, of some three hundred acres.

Angus, completed his schooling in Yass and also Canberra, as Yass had no suitable high school for Angus. He completed an apprenticeship and became a carpenter, after some time he attended the Canberra College of Advanced Education and completed Applied Science in building, and became a building inspector with the Department of Housing and Construction in Canberra.

He hated the Yass climate and moved to Cairns in Far North Queensland, where he found employment there as a building surveyor. His parents sold their property and retired to a village with aged care facilities in Canberra. They passed in the same year that Angus had turned sixty and that inheritance had caused Angus's decision to retire at the age of sixty.

Angus enjoyed Cairns and its climate and lived in the Northern Beach suburb of Clifton Beach, where he met his future wife Lynette. It wasn't really a chance meeting, but rather a slightly unusual meeting.

Angus had returned home from work one afternoon to discover his unit at Clifton Beach, had been broken into, items appeared to have been stolen, such as an old watch that no longer worked, a camera, that also no longer worked, and about one thousand dollars in cash from his bedroom drawer, but what annoyed him was that the contents of his fridge, which was mainly beer, had been drunk and the bottles scattered around the unit.

He had called the police who advised that, as it was not urgent, they would send someone around tomorrow, at ten o'clock in the morning. That evening, Angus took a cab to the Reef Casino in town and had dinner. He then had a bit of a play on the poker machines and started talking to a rather attractive, tall woman with short hair. He offered to buy her a drink and she said, OK, another beer, thanks. He left the Casino a little later and said that it was nice meeting you to the young lady, who said her name was Lynette.

Angus was patiently waiting for the police at ten o'clock the next morning, as he had been advised. At around, ten forty five, two plain clothes police officers knocked on his door, Angus let them in and, as they were introducing themselves, the female police officer said "Gus! Fancy meeting you here, that was great last night ". And, the rest is history.

They are now both retired and happily living on the Esplanade in Cairns City.

Gus got out of bed and checked the time, it was seven thirty. He went to the bathroom and emerged about ten minutes later and walked out to the front balcony to where Lynette was sitting having breakfast. He told her about the call..

Lynette was ecstatic, asking "he didn't say how much!"
"No, he just said it was very substantial, he didn't really expand on the value, just said sole beneficiary".
"Yahoo, let's go" replied Lynette.

The offices of Wedderburn & Holt, are located in Denham Street, Townsville.
So, as Gus, lived with his wife, Lynette, in a unit on the Esplanade, in Cairns City, an appointment was set for the following week. Gus had to attend to the transfer of the estate to him, including the transfer of the title of the property, of the late Mr Teague, and cash in the bank of some six hundred and ninety two thousand dollars, to be transferred to Gus's bank account.

During the transfer process, Malcolm Davies told Gus that Mr Teague's wife, Sonia Teague, had already challenged the will, but it was to no avail unless the beneficiary as named in the will could not be found or was dead.

It would seem that the bottom line was, that Uncle Lachlan, had cut his wife out of his will as there was no mention of her and all land titles were in the name of Lachlan Teague only, there was no shared interest or other shares in common. Interesting, thought Gus, but who cares, its all mine now, stiff shit to Mrs Sonia thought Gus, and shared his views with his wife.

Whilst waiting for a full inventory of all goods and chattels of the property to be printed, Gus asked Malcolm how well had he known his uncle, and was quite astonished to discover that the one and only time that Lachlan Teague had been into their office, was to make his will about six months prior to his death. Did Malcolm know the cause of death, Lynette had asked casually, but Malcolm could not answer, and said that he had assumed natural causes.

After a while, the title was transferred, 'all done!" The property known as 'Woolgar River Park', of approximately 30,000Ha / 73,000 Acres located in the County of Yappar and Parish of Saxby, on the Woolgar River, and about 150km North West of Hughenden, there was also the main homestead, which is a two story, five bedroom home with verandahs on three sides, a cool room to one side of the residence and a four car garage attached.

Other accommodation on the property is a three bedroom, two bathroom, Managers house located approximately one hundred and sixty meters from the homestead and two separate, fully self contained staff quarters of two bedrooms each, one is located adjacent to the manager's house and the other at approximately four kilometres from the homestead.

There are numerous bores on the property all of an approximate depth of three hundred metres, there are also Riparian water rights on the Woolgar River. There are shaded cattle yards on the property which has a carrying capacity of 6000 backgrounders (cattle).

There was no mention of any stock present on the property at the time of the will, but accordingly, if there is stock on the property that belongs to the property and is not owned by another lea-see of the property then they form part of the estate.

The property description is from when it was purchased by Mr Teague in 2003.

But unfortunately, there were no keys to the buildings on the property. The only keys the solicitor had were the keys to the front gates that they had organised to be locked to stop any trespassers. It was not known if Mrs Sonia Teague had vacated the property, they had assumed she had followed the notice to quit the property and take only her personal possessions. Malcolm had added, that even her car was in Lachlan's name and she had to leave it at the property.

The inventory was passed to Malcolm from his secretary, and Malcolm handed a copy to Gus.

It started with the property as described in the county and parish, complete with section number and geographical location and description and went on to list all furniture and furnishings inside the residence and all machinery, tools and equipment that was in the various outbuildings, It gave a description of motor vehicles that were or should be about the property.

2012 BMW X5, with registration number, 2018 Honda Accord Euro, with registration number, 2006 Toyota Landcruiser Cab/chassis with steel tray body, with registration number.

Malcolm also told Gus that it was also his companies responsibility, to check the accuracy of the inventory prior to the beneficiary signing the acknowledgement and that he would be happy to accompany Gus out to the property on an agreeable and mutual date, however, as the property is some Five hundred and sixty kilometres from Townsville, he suggested they stay the night at Hughenden which is around one hundred and fifty miles from the property.

Gus thanked Malcolm for his help and suggested dinner that evening, and perhaps we can discuss a day to head out and check the property. Sadly, Malcolm said he could not this evening as he is having a BBQ that afternoon at his house with his parents who are visiting Townsville, but, why don't you come to the BBQ and we can discuss the dates further?

That afternoon, at Malcolm's house at North Ward, Gus and Lynette, were introduced to Malcolm's wife Ros and to Malcolm's mother and father. Gus had brought a carton of XXXX Gold stubbies and a bottle of Port Phillip Estate Chardonnay, which he didn't have a clue about.
A great BBQ was enjoyed and much of the talk was about retirement and living in a unit. Malcolm and Ros didn't have children and Gus, nor Lynette did not ask why, and soon Malcolm's mother and father declared it was their bedtime, and left the other four to get acquainted.

It didn't take Ros very long at all to mention that we must be so excited and that she wished she could get a call out of the blue like they had received, so then they started chatting about the event over another drink, or four!
Malcolm revealed that his company receives all death notices and they check their files accordingly, when Gus's uncle's name came up as registered with Wedderburn and Holt, Mal's name was on the file reference so it came to him.

As soon as he saw the name, Malcolm remembered the man. He had come in out of the blue and had asked the receptionist if he could get a will made up. The receptionist told him that he would have to make an appointment, and he would also require three types of identification, including at least one type with a photograph and if real estate was involved in the will, he would require a rates notice in his name and also an electricity account invoice, in his name.

The man had said that he had all the required information in his bag with him and he said he was from out of town. He had said, it doesn't matter and was about to leave when the receptionist told the man to wait for a moment and she would check. As fate would have it, Malcolm had a cancellation and although he did have another appointment, he could squeeze in Mr Lachlan Teague.

Ros got more drinks as this story was getting good. Malcolm continued, he was fairly quiet, and said he wanted to make a will, a simple will with one benefactor. Malcolm had asked for his details and other information about the contents of the will, it was then that Lachlan Teague produced the inventory of his estate that he wanted to leave to his nephew, Angus Teague of Australia.

He had also produced, with this inventory, a copy of original documents, including land title and deed to his property and deeds for goods and chattels and vehicles, all in his name.

Malcolm had advised Lachlan Teague that he would require more information with respect to Angus's address, but Lachlan had said that was all he knew with respect to Angus's address, however, he could offer Angus's birthdate and Angus's father's name if that would help.

Malcolm had the will completed and Lachlan Teague had signed it whilst his secretary had witnessed it. He had then paid the required fees including a 'hand over' additional fee which included an allowance for travel and accommodation.

This time, Gus got up to get more drinks, thinking, how strange!
When Gus returned with drinks all around, Malcolm continued. The strange thing is, as everyone went silent when we got notification of the death, we went to register the execution of the will only to discover that another will had been registered only two hours before the will we held. But when they checked the wills currency, our's was valid and the other will,.. was void!

Well, Mrs Teague,..oops, sorry Lynette, I meant to say, Mrs Sonia Teague came storming into our office the very same day, demanding to know more about the will, and then, as we told you earlier today, she challenged the will, she lost on will currency dates, then demanded she have at least half, but when we produced the inventory together with titles and deeds, she was "fucked", so to speak, oops, pardon the French. Another strange thing Gus, is that when she asked who the benefactor was, and I told her, she said she had never heard of such a person.

Malcom asked Gus and Lynette, what day they would like to go up to the property to have a look and they responded that any time suited them, the sooner the better as they were really keen to have a look. Gus suggested that they all travel up there and make a holiday out of it, Ros said that would be good as Malcolm's mum and dad are here, then they could look after the dog while they are away." Let's do it". Malcolm suggested the day after tomorrow, that's a Thursday, we can have Thursday and Friday at Hughenden and come back Saturday, Done!....another drink?

Wednesday morning, Gus and Lynette were staying at the Townsville Casino and had decided to spend some of their newfound wealth, that had been transferred into their bank account overnight.
They had only come down to Townsville for one night and had brought very little in clothing and now as it seemed it would be at least four days before they got home, they went to Castletown shopping centre.

Thursday morning at eight o'clock, Malcolm and Ros collected Gus and Lynette, from the steps of the Townsville Casino in Malcolm's Landcruiser 200, VX. Ros moved from the front seat and sat in the back with Lynette, to enable the men to talk about business, Ros handed out cold bottles of water to both Gus and Lynette. Malcolm asked Gus if his car was ok in the Casino's car park for a few days, and Gus said," It's insured."

The conversation was mainly about what Gus and Lynette were up to in Cairns, and what did they use to do. Lynette told Ros that Gus was a building surveyor until his, early retirement, last year at the grand age of sixty, but still works on occasions when his former workplace calls him in from time to time. Lynette continued that she was formally a detective sergeant, with the Qld police, but retired when Gus did so last year.

Malcolm asked Gus how well he knew his uncle Lachlan, it's a long story Malcolm replied Gus. I haven't seen him since I left Scotland when I was ten years old. That's exactly fifty years ago this year, he was fifteen years younger than my dad, and from a different mother. Let me work it out, Dad died at eighty six and that was six years ago, which would have made Lachlan, seventy seven when he died so he would have been twenty-seven years old when I last saw him.

Gus went on to say that his father, Alisdair, had an adjoining property in Canonbie with his father Campbell Teague, and his father's brother, Lachlan had an adjoining property on the other side of Gus's father's property. "Have I totally confused everybody?" asked Gus.

Anyway, my dad's property was a gift from his dad, as was Lachlan's, and they all worked in fine together and all made good money.

But, my father was fed up with sheep and decided to produce Aberdeen Angus cattle on his property. So much to my grandfather's disgust, that it caused such a fight, so my father resorted back to the sheep.

But my father had lost interest and had decided to migrate to Australia and he asked his father to buy his property from him. His father got the shits and told Alisdair, that if he left he would disown him and cut him off completely.

Gus finished the story with, there was no reason for the old man to get like that, but that is the way it went in Scotland.

They stopped in Charters Towers for morning tea then kept on to Hughenden. Malcolm was musing on the way there, whether Mrs Sonia Teague may still be there? "she shouldn't be", he said, as the court order to quit was served to her hand delivered and receipted so if she is, it might be interesting!.

They stopped off for lunch at Hughenden, then checked into the Royal Hotel-Motel, in Moran Street. They then headed off toward Richmond, turning left just after Richmond, onto the Richmond Woolgar Road, then about thirty five kilometres along that road, then another turn right for about six kilometres and they came to a grid in the road with a gate, beside the grid was another big, double gate, for road trains they supposed, with the name on one side of the timber fencing 'Woolgar River Park' that needed to be repainted badly.

Mrs Sonia Teague

Both the large gates were locked together with a chain and padlocks and the single gate on the grid was also locked by a chain and a padlock. Malcolm fumbled in the console for the gate keys, found them and got out of the car and joined Gus at the grid gate, "what great looking country", Gus said to no one in particular as Malcolm was attempting to open the lock. "No good" he said to Gus, "the key won't work, I'll try the double gates, but same thing" Malcolm said whilst trying to open the double gates.

The locks have been changed again since we had them changed, as it was supposed to be the same key for both locks, and these locks are entirely different from each other.

Gus had been looking at the grid gate, the hinges were just pins that were welded to the gate and fit into sockets that were welded on the steel post, and he discovered he could lift the gate up and lift the pins out of the sockets, then using the chain and padlock as a hinge, he could swing the gate away from the grid. "You Ripper" called Malcolm, whilst also observing fairly fresh tyre tracks through the grid gate, and on both sides.

They drove slowly from the gates to the house, which was about another two kilometres, they came around a long curve in the track and the house appeared with its full length verandah and a large Porte Cocheres in the centre. Gus and Lynette just looked at the house in awe.

In the centre of the Porte-cochere, were double doors with extravagant mouldings, that were securely locked and a stroll around the whole perimeter revealed only securely locked doors and windows. As they all stood under the grand entry, wondering their next move, Ros bent over to a concrete, empty plant pot and tilted it to one side, revealing a key, which drew applause from the others watching.

They were just about to try the key when the noise of a car in the driveway disturbed them and all looked toward the driveway, to see a white Landcruiser ute, driven by a large man with dark hair, pull up next to Malcolm's cruiser. The man remained in the car, just staring at the people at the house entrance. A woman, seated on the passenger side, and somewhat obscured, got from the vehicle and walked to the front of the vehicle screaming, "Who are you, what do you want, who are you"

Gus, a little shocked by the woman's attitude had actually thought that this may happen and had prepared himself, well somewhat, prepared himself, and simply said "I beg your pardon, Madam, and who, may I ask, are YOU!"
Gus's words had stopped her dead, Gus could hardly believe it, but somehow, knew exactly what she was going to say next, he hoped. "I am the OWNER of this property" the

woman spat, with self indigence, "NO MADAM, you are NOT, this is my property and you are trespassing.

Malcolm, got in then before the woman could return a response, "Excuse me, are you, by any chance Mrs Sonia Teague?"
"What concern is it to you, if I am, who are you people and what do you want, and what do you mean when you say, you are the owner of this property, it belongs to me!", starting to calm.

Malcolm, introduced himself and then Angus Teague, and went on to explain that she was in fact trespassing and that she should not be on this property, as it was now owned by Mr Angus Teague, who was today taking formal possession of this property, today, now in fact.

Well, this was the last straw for Mrs Sonia Teague, who called to the driver of the ute and told him to come inside the house with her, as she reached for the concrete pot plant, only to realise the key was not in place.

Can we please discuss this in a sensible manner, tried Gus, but the woman simply glared at him, so Gus thought, you, "bitch". He was not here to put up with this shit!
Gus turned to Malcolm and said he was not putting up with this behaviour "What do we do now, I want her off this property now", continued Gus. He was now becoming both angry and upset with this woman, whereas, earlier he was

actually looking forward to meeting her, she was, after all, his aunty. But not now!

The woman, upon hearing Gus, said that no one, no one is going to move her from her home, she knew her rights and she could actually call squatters rights and remain here.
Malcolm told her that unfortunately, for herself, in this instance she had been served a court order to remove herself from the property and failing to do so, could render her to be arrested, for not complying with that order. She remained indifferent, so Malcolm said they were going to bring in the police and have her removed. He then suggested to Ros, Lynette and Gus, that they go back to Hughenden and enlist the police to remove this woman from the property.

It was a tense drive back to Hughenden, to the police station. They arrived at approximately two thirty. It was a fairly large building on Brodie Street, Malcolm and Gus went into the station, fortunately, Malcolm had come armed with a copy of the court order together with the receipt of it duly served to Mrs Sonia Teague.

The acting sergeant, Trevor Strawn, having read the order, asked if the woman was still on the property and upon Malcolm's confirmation, said he would need to get a policewoman from Charters Towers, to assist in the removal in the case, as it may become physical.

The sergeant then contacted Charters Towers Police, who confirmed that a WPC would be at their disposal tomorrow morning at ten o'clock.

The Teague's, and the Davies, enjoyed dinner that night at the Royal Hotel and a few drinks afterwards, as they discussed what a fairly disappointing day it had turned into as all were looking forward to having a good look around the property, but it had been a big day, and was going to be a fairly busy day tomorrow also, by the looks of it.
The bet was, that the coppers would most likely arrest Mrs Sonia Teague tomorrow, well, we'll see.
Why she had to act in such an aggressive manner, was beyond everyone, it could have all been sorted out amicably, Malcolm suggested

At ten am the next morning, they all gathered at the police station, the lady officer had arrived from Charters Towers and was in deep conversation with Sergeant Trevor Strawn.
The Sergeant said he would see everybody out there and he left on his own in his police sedan, the lady officer and another male constable headed out in a hi lux paddy wagon. Malcolm's car followed the two police cars.

The gate over the grid was again locked, so Gus did his trick, they all proceeded to the front door of the house. The white landcruiser was parked under the Porte-cochere and the front door opened as they all drove up.

Mrs Sonia Teague emerged from the porte-cochere and welcomed the party with a big friendly, "Hello, well, hello, how nice to see visitors, what on earth is the occasion for this"

Sergeant Strawn did not respond to Mrs Sonia's hello and simply said. "Are you Sonia Teague"
"Well, yes, of course I am, what is…"
Strawn cut her off, "You have to leave this property immediately, in accordance with the court order number, issued at Townsville district court, you should leave now, if you do not leave of your own free will, you will be escorted from this property, if you resist you may be arrested".

Sonia just glared at the Sergeant, then said she will get her things together and will be out by this evening. Too late for that I am afraid, any items that were not removed by the date of your order to quit, now become the property of the legal owner of this property, if you do not leave now, you will be escorted.

Gus, intervened," Really Sergeant, is this necessary, surely she can get her"…..
Gus was cut off by the Sergeant, "Sir, you have instructed, that the Qld police to act upon an issued court order, we can only follow the protocol as laid down for us by the law courts",
Malcolm, also butted in, "At least let her pack a bag Sergeant".

The sergeant agreed to Malcolm's request and told the police women to accompany Mrs Teague to pack one bag, then to write a list of personal items she would like to request to have returned by the legal owner of the property, which he may agree or disagree.

After only a brief period of time, Mrs Sonia Teague emerged from the house with a small suitcase on wheels, there were no tears streaming down her face, only hatred in her eyes as she stopped and left the case at the Porte-cochere and walked across the driveway to open one of the garage doors located at the end of the house, when the police sergeant again addressed her to ask where she thought she might be going.

To which Mrs Sonia Teague responded with an indignant "to get my car" as she disappeared into the garage, soon to drive from the garage in a Honda Accord.

As she stopped the car in front of the Porte-cochere, Malcolm told her that was not her car to take, Gus, again intervened, saying she could have the car, just get off the property.
Malcolm warned Gus not to be so quick to give things away, Gus just waved him down and said I just want her gone from here, the sergeant agreed with Gus, adding that she would have required some form of transportation and suggested he transfer the vehicle registration at Hughenden when practicable.

Mrs Sonia Teague put the bag on the back seat of the Honda, slammed the back door, glared at Gus and Malcolm, and then said "You will hear from me", she got into the driver's seat and took off rapidly.

All sighed a relief, and the sergeant commented, "That was too easy, watch out for that one fellows", as he turned to leave with the other constables.

"Thank heavens for that", Malcolm said as they all slowly walked to the front door, looking forward to exploring.

Woolgar River Park

The entrance of the homestead of Woolgar River Park is quite impressive, with its large, formal entrance vestibule. The polished timber and stainless steel staircase in the centre and towards the end of the vestibule looks quite splendid. A large, open reception room is to the left of the entrance area and double doors are to the right that leads to a large lounge room, with a dining area to its rear and a door to the massive kitchen leading from this. A serverey is also adjacent to the dining area. In the right hand corner of the lounge room beside a large bay window, that looks out across the plains, is a curved bar with six bar stools. There is also a round, low table with four, lay back chairs. There is also a restroom beside the bar.

A large, open fireplace is in the centre of the lounge, with a round hearth surrounding the metal base, and a large circular copper chimney with a huge circular flange is above the fireplace. There are two, three seater, square design lounges that face each other to one side of the fireplace and another two similar lounges in one corner and a wall mounted television. A three quarter size pool table was placed in the adjacent corner, opposite the bar with a magnificent looking corner cue rack.

The reception room contains a long table and six timber and leather, office-type chairs, and two other, office type three-seater lounges, there is another door leading to an office with a fairly simple looking desk and chair and a window looking out to the out buildings around the property.

On the desk was a Mac Desktop computer, a wireless keyboard and a wireless mouse. A solitary, two door filing cabinet was behind the desk.

A framed, aerial view of the property was on the wall opposite the window.

Another door in the reception room also led to a restroom. There were no bedrooms on this level.

The kitchen was certainly overkill, to which they all agreed, before moving into the kitchen store or more like a butler's pantry that had another door exiting to a corridor that led out to the rear door.

On this corridor was also a door to the laundry. The laundry was a large room with all the associated laundry items including a steam ironing machine, another store room and a cold room. There was also a set of stairs leading to the upper level in the corner. Pretty flash, to say the least, was the general consensus as they moved to the stairwell in the laundry.

The laundry stairs ended on the upper level with a small landing and a door that led to the main hallway with spotted gum timber polished flooring to the left, and a full size window to the right, this window allowed daylight through to meet the daylight coming from the other end of the hallway by the front stairway and front window. Wow, they all seemed to mutter, as each came onto the upper level.

There were three doors to the right side of the hall and two doors to the left, with an open lounge area at the top of the front stairs, containing a three seat lounge, two chairs and a television and a doorway leading to yet another, rest room.

The three doors on the right were bedrooms each with a queen size bed, built in robe, one lounge type looking chair and an ensuite complete with bath, shower and toilet. They were all pretty much identical with the exception of a small desk and chair and nothing really special, quite ordinary.

One of the two doors on the other side was the master bedroom, there was lots of daylight from two windows on each side of a super king size bed, a double reclining lounge and a single reclining chair and a television, a desk in a corner with another Mac desktop computer and a swivel chair.
A much bigger ensuite in this room that also contained a spa and double opposed showers.

The last door on this level led to another bedroom that was almost identical to the master bedroom but, this one with a king size bed and no desk, but two lounge type chairs and a television. This room was just a little smaller in room size than the master bedroom.

The first thing that they all noticed was that there were no signs of anyone living there, on the beds were only mattresses, all the wardrobes were empty, and nothing in the drawers or inside the wardrobes.

The kitchen was as clean as a new house, there were no saucepans or frypans, the cupboards were empty, no crockery or cutlery. There was nothing, it seemed as if the whole house had been cleaned out. Weird!!. The only items they could see were bits and pieces, such as some glasses in the bar, and a knife block in the kitchen, but no knives.

They checked out the other house, its front door on the wide verandah was unlocked and someone had definitely been living here recently or still was. It was the station manager's house, they assumed. It had a lounge with a combined kitchen and dining room, an ensuite in the main bedroom and a separate bathroom with a separate toilet and it had three bedrooms and a laundry on the back verandah.

There was no clothing in any of the robes, but items of food in the kitchen cupboards, dirty plates in the sink and some crockery and cutlery in the drawers including saucepans and frypans. A green track suit top lay on the lounge and a pair of very old sneakers were on the verandah next to the laundry and a dog food bowl that appeared half empty, there was also an ashtray with several, hand rolled buts.

The garage, a four car garage with four roller doors, contained the X5 beamer, no other vehicles were in the garage, and there was no entry to the house from the garage. Then, what appeared to be the workshop, contained only a bench, there were no tools or equipment, just a bare concrete floor.

What was thought, could be a machinery shed, was totally empty, nothing.

Chook shed, nothing. Dog kennels, nothing.

Gus looked around at the adjoining paddocks and said out loud that he supposed there was no stock on the property either. They all agreed it was weird. And that it looked as if it had been stripped of everything since Lachlan died, but why, what was going on?

As Malcolm and Gus compared items in the inventory against physical items, it showed many small items to be missing, such as wall decorations, here and there, other items such as a piano, a gun cabinet with two rifles, a .222 Stirling, a .308 Sako and a five shot, pump action shotgun. There was also a printer missing from the office and a wall mounted key cabinet, complete with keys and a second two door filing cabinet were also missing.

The inventory included a John Deere gator, A John Deere 6430 tractor with a front end loader and other attachments, a John Deere 2420 with a centre mower, and a Husqvarna 542X front mower. All were missing from the property with other minor items like hand tools and power tools, chainsaws, whipper snippers and hedges.

There was no mention of stock or any other animals in the inventory, as the property had not, according to Lachlan when he made up the inventory, been trading for over a year. Malcolm was very annoyed at the missing items that amounted to many thousand dollars and that he would see Sergeant Trevor Strawn tomorrow with respect to theft.

Gus told Malcolm that it does not matter, Gus was over the moon with property as it was and he could not care about the missing gear and he certainly did not want the police involved.

Lynette agreed, she too was over the moon and couldn't care less about the missing stuff and suggested they lock up what they can lock up here and go back to Hughenden for a drink before, she dies, she said. They walked around the property and locked whatever they could then headed back to Hughenden.

It was only two thirty when they arrived back at the Royal Hotel, Gus rang around for a locksmith but there was none in Hughenden, the closest being Charters Towers, who said he could be there around nine o'clock tomorrow. Gus said he would call back in a few minutes to confirm and asked Malcolm if they could extend their stay in Hughenden for another day. "We would love to", said Ros, "I'll ring Malcolm's mum now and let her know". Gus confirmed tomorrow with the locksmith.

Over drinks, the conversation was, what will we do, should we live there, should we get it going again with cattle, what, and more whats. Malcom suggested that Gus should get someone out there pronto to watch the place as he did not trust Sonia, everyone agreed. Lynette went to the bar for more drinks and, while she was there chatting to the girl behind the bar, who sounded like a pommy backpacker, she asked if she knew anyone who might like a caretaking job at a farm out of town for a while?.

Lynette had hit the jackpot, the girl behind the bar said that her girlfriend and her male partner were leaving here tomorrow as they could not find any suitable work in Hughenden, she said she would ask them if Lynette wanted. Lynette asked how soon could she ask them, the bar girl said that they normally come in for a drink about now and that she would look out for them.

Lynette returned to the table and, as she passed the drinks, she told of the conversation with the girl behind the bar. Before she could complete the conversation, the girl from the bar approached them with two other people in tow. The girl addressed Lynette and said "These are the people I was telling you about" and she added, "Do you want three caretakers, I've had enough of working behind a bar, I came to Australia to see the sun and get a tan, not stuck behind a bar".

Lynette did not hesitate to answer with a distinct yes! To the bar girl, let's all talk.

The bar girl, whose name they discovered was Janice, introduced her girlfriend Hailee and Hailee's partner, Willem, then said she could not talk until another one hour when she would finish work, but said she was super keen.

Bloody hell, thought Lynette, we don't even know what we are going to pay these people or anything, and here we are employing people.

Lynette, introduced Hailee and Willem to everybody and Malcolm got more chairs, Gus asked what they would like to drink, and went for more drinks.

Willem, a big strapping looking lad with fair hair, was from Valkenswaard, a country town near the city of Eindhoven in the Netherlands, where his parents breed goats.

Hailee was from Bramley, south of London UK. They had been in Australia for six months and had their own transport.

Malcolm, took over, like solicitors tend to, and explained the available position at Woolgar River Park, he explained that at this stage there was not really any work to do out there, but just to be there and make sure no strangers came on to the property, basically just the house's and the outbuildings, they didn't have to go checking the paddocks.

When they were told that the accommodation was a three bedroom house, they were delighted and keen to go.

Lynette.. jumped in with, there will be lots of cleaning and maybe some painting coming up, and mowing and a bit of

gardening. Gus added that we would pay cash, of course, much to Malcolm's disapproval. They explained that they needed them to start tomorrow, which was fine with them.
Janice had finished work and brought drinks over to the table for everyone, and the job details were repeated along with the accommodation and that was alright sharing the house with her friends, of course, she said, but said she could not go there until she had finished at the pub in a week's time. Willem and Hailee said they would come in and pick her up in a week's time.

All done, directions on how to get to Woolgar River Park, were given to the new staff and that they would meet tomorrow at nine o clock. Things were starting to look better, they said their goodbyes to Janice, Hailee and Willem and went for dinner.

The conversation that evening over dinner and more drinks was, of course, Woolgar River Park, and also the strange, Sonia Teague!

"It was evident", mentioned Lynette, "that Sonia was not living in the house, so where was she living and why did she appear at the property when she did on that first day they all arrived there"?
"And"! Said Ros, "who was the bloke in the Landcruiser with her".
"And" continued Lynette, "why was the place devoid of any items, you know, nothing, it looked like no one has lived

there for quite a time. Didn't Lachlan die at home, in his bed, where are all his clothes, it just seems strange to me".

"Should we sell it, or live in it" Lynette, asked Gus, then to Malcolm, "What do you reckon it would be worth"?

Malcolm had a think, and suggested, off hand, "Four million, maybe five, I really don't know, but it would not be too hard to find out", Malcolm said. But Lynette responded pretty quickly with a "no, no not yet, let's think about it, there is no rush, not now, once we get our caretakers in place and it might be nice to live there, it is a beautiful house". "But a fucking long way away from anything" added Gus.

They all left at seven the next morning to arrive at the property by nine that morning, they overtook an old Subaru Outback that contained Willem and Hailee, they all waved as they passed.

The gate at the grid was still closed as Gus had left it upon departing yesterday afternoon and there did not seem to be any fresh tyre tracks, but they were uncertain. As they pulled up in front of the house, Malcolm, having a sudden thought and remembering that Sonia had come from inside the house when they all arrived yesterday, wondered how did she get in, as Ros had taken the key from the plant pot and had not given it to Sonia. Sonia did not have a key as she had looked for her key under the plant pot. He reminded Gus of this and they agreed to look for the way that she had, obviously, broken in. Good thinking Malcolm, Gus also said he would ask the locksmith to also look for a way to break in, whilst changing the locks this morning.

They all looked, apprehensibly up the driveway as another vehicle approached, a landcruiser troopy with sign writing, it was the locksmith, and not too far behind him were Willem and Hailee.

Gus introduced himself to the locksmith and his off sider, whom he had brought along as it may be a bigger job than he had expected, it was looking that way the locksmith thought.

Dave, said the locksmith, outstretching his arm towards Gus, and this is my number one man Grant. Gus started walking them both toward the house saying he wanted a master key for every lock on the place and separate pass keys for the main house, the manager's house, the machinery shed, the equipment shed and the entrance gates.

He also wanted a restricted key system for the control of the number of keys produced, two keys each for all pass keys, except the manager's house which shall be three keys. And three master keys. Could you also check for a break in around the main house as you go about, as he thought someone had broken in the other night and he did not know where?

As an afterthought, Gus asked the locksmith if he could produce keys to the BMW. The locksmith said he could get a new transponder for it sometime next week if he can get a code number from the owner's logbook. Gus said he would look for it.

Lynette and Ros were showing the caretakers the manager's house and they were going through the cupboards throwing out old food that was out of date and other items that were broken or of no use. They had opened the refrigerator door to allow it to air a little. The caretakers said they had enough food to last them until next Thursday when they would pick up Janice from Hughenden and also do some shopping.
They had bedding and pillows in their Outback that would be fine for their bedroom in the house but they thought Janice might have to buy some sheets and blankets.
The caretakers were very pleased with their new job and accommodation and started to unpack their car.

Malcolm and Ros had really nothing more to do around the homestead, neither did Lynette or Gus for that matter, but Gus could not leave until the locksmith had finished and had handed him the keys. The locksmith had estimated about one o'clock he should have it all done, other than the BMW.

Malcolm suggested they could all go for a drive around the property but they would not really know which way to go, the parish plan only shows an outline on a larger map, but no detail.
Gus suggested that he would see if he could get some topographical maps when he gets back to Cairns and that

they could all spend a few days up here discovering the property

Ros and Malcolm thought that would be a great idea and Lynette said she would be bringing up linen for the beds and crockery, cutlery and saucepans, food, drinks and good heavens knows what else from Cairns in the next week or so, to make the place a home.

Gus suggested to Malcolm that if he and Ros wanted to head back to Hughenden, instead of having to wait around for the locksmith, Gus and Lynette would bring the Landcruiser into Hughenden and leave it there for Janice to bring back. "Sounds good" said Malcolm, 'will you be right with it, we'd best make sure it's a goer'.

It was getting on in years, being a 2006 model, but the Landcruiser was in excellent condition other than the dirt on the outside, the inside was very clean and had been well looked after and it was registered for another four months. But! No keys.

The locksmith, responding to yet another request wandered over and opened the glove box, here to his delight and still enclosed in its plastic cover, the owner's manual where Dave found the key number and produced a key in minutes. It reminded Gus that he was going to look for the BMW's log book and he was now confident after seeing the Landcruiser's log books intact that the beamers would be also. The locksmith suggested he recode the Landcruiser locks as someone must have keys and could return and take the Landcruiser. "Great Idea Dave", said Gus.

The Landcruiser started instantly but showed only a quarter of a tank of fuel. "The fuel tank on the stand"! said Malcolm, "Let's check it out". It was located out of view, beside the machinery shed and the visigauge on the front of the tank showed over three quarters full. It had a brand new padlock on the delivery handle that had just been placed there by the locksmith. Things were looking good, at last.

It was eleven o'clock when Ros and Malcolm left Woolgar River Park to head back to Hughenden, Gus said he and Lynette should be there about three o'clock, just in time for afternoon drinks, as they waved them off.

Both Lynette and Gus were happy to be alone to have another look at the house and make plans and quite a huge list of items to bring on their next visit, although they had only briefly discussed it, they were going to move into the house within the next couple of weeks whilst leaving their Cairns unit for long weekends and holidays. It was just so exciting!!

Lynette had ideas of getting the girls, Hailee and Janice, to clean the house while they were away, but after another look at the house, she decided she did not want other people in there while she was absent, besides it was not really dirty at all.

They went and saw the caretakers, to tell them that they would leave the Landcruiser at Hughenden for Janice to bring back. Gus presumed she had a license. Gus also told Willem that he would organise a ride on mower for him in Hughenden, together with some fuel drums for petrol for the mower, that he could pick up with the Landcruiser when they go to Hughenden on Thursday. Willem thought Janice may have a license, but if not either himself or Hailee could drive the cruiser back.

Gus told Willem and Hailee that he would go to an ATM in Hughenden and leave a couple of weeks pay for each of them, in cash as agreed, with Janice in Hughenden, if that was fine with them. Hailee said that's cool, she trusted Janice with her life. Gus went on to say that he and Lynette would be back in about two weeks, he gave Willem his and Lynette's mobile numbers and told them not to hesitate to call either of them. Gus then acquired both Willem's and Hailee's mobile numbers and said he would text them Malcolm's mobile number when he got it from Malcolm later that day.

The locksmith had finished and fortunately, the locksmith's portable EFTPOS machine's service was with Telstra, the only mobile reception in the area. Gus received all the keys he had requested and had given Dave his home address to mail the new BMW transponder key that he would organise from the code they had found in the BMW's owner's log book that was in the console of the car.

As the locksmith left, he asked if he and his mates could come out pigging, sometime in the future, Gus told him anytime and reminded Dave that he had Gus's mobile, just give me a call Gus said

They went and said goodbye to Willem and Hailee, who were busy cleaning the fridge and oven in the manager's house, they were just so happy when Gus gave them two keys to the manager's house and one key each to the machinery shed and gates. Gus told Willem to take it easy and we would see you in two weeks, then after that, we should be able to get organised but in the interim, just watch out for the place, keep it neat and enjoy. Gus told Willem that the locksmith had put the grid gate back on its pivots and that he could leave it open during the day if he wished and lock it at night, it was up to him.

Lynette and Gus waved goodbye to the caretakers and drove off in the Landcruiser and over the grid towards Hughenden.

It was the worst trip as far as comfort went in the Landcruiser ute, talk about bounce, it seemed about ninety five to a hundred was as fast as they could go without being thrown from the seat, maybe because it had no weight on the back they thought, or maybe the tyres are pumped up too high.

They arrived in Hughenden at three thirty, parked at the Hotel and went straight to the bar.

Janice was working at the bar and was full of questions about the property, what did Willem and Hailee think, were Willem and Hailee happy? Janice finally got a couple of beers for them. Gus had the third key for the manager's house and a gate key in his pocket and also the Landcruiser key. He retrieved them and gave them to Janice while telling her about the Landcruiser parked in the motel car park, Janice got even more excited and said she was going to call Hailee when she finished work.

Gus went to the ATM at the hotel and withdrew two weeks' pay each for Willem and Hailee and one week's pay for Janice, which he gave to Janice to pass on the other two's pay when she sees them on Thursday. He told Janice that they would see her in a couple of weeks, have fun.

Gus then called the mower centre and organised a Zorro zero turn mower and two twenty litre fuel drums, he paid with his credit card.

Lynette and Gus then went to their room for a well deserved shower before meeting Ros and Malcolm for drinks and dinner. It was back in Townsville tomorrow.

Another dinner at the hotel, and lots of conversation about Woolgar Creek Park, and also Sonia Teague.

Ros asked if we had noticed on Friday, the day the police had gone out there, that Sonia did not even look upset about having to move from the house, also that she had stuff all luggage when she left, not to mention that there were no sheets or blankets on any of the beds. Her small suitcase was nowhere near big enough for sheets, let alone a blanket and a pillow.

"I think", said Ros, "that she had only arrived there that morning and who was that guy that we saw driving the Landcruiser on the Thursday"?

Everyone agreed with Ros, Sonia did not seem to have been upset, certainly looked like she was full of hate. She walked out of the front doors on the Friday, but how did she get in?

Gus volunteered that the locksmith had found no signs of forced entry, but had found marks on the pavers near the laundry door that indicated that a large pot had been moved, another key, suggested Malcolm.

"

The Landcruiser was parked in the Porte-cochere", commented Lynette," it was not parked there when we left on Thursday, it was in the driveway and the the fellow driving it was not present on Friday, so I think that Sonia had arrived only that morning to remove something from the house and was about to leave when we all turned up".

"I'll bet the keys to the Landcruiser were in her pocket" Ros supposed.

"When we walked around the house, did anyone try lifting the garage doors", asked Malcolm.

"I did", responded Gus, "I remember now that I definitely did as I remember trying all four doors as I thought the garage may be another entrance to the house, but they were all locked".

"Yes", Malcolm continued," but Sonia did not unlock the garage door she opened to get the Honda, it was already unlocked".

More pondering by all, whilst sipping on more drinks, "And you know what", said Lynette as Gus grinned to himself, Lynette was forever saying "And you know what" he just had to grin.
No one else said it so Gus did, "No! What!"
Everybody had a bit of a laugh, except Lynette who went on to ask the question, "Why was the place cleaned out of everything, other than furniture"?

Hmmm, they were all thinking, was Lachlan's body in the house for a long period that everything was contaminated, no because the mattresses were still on the beds, they would have been the first things to go, surely. Memories, did Sonia have too many memories of Lachlan that she had to remove items? What, like pots and pans, come on. And, what about the machinery? What happened to that, sold, stolen?

All in all just too many questionable things and, no answers, quite bewildering and it seemed the more drinks they had, the more bewildered they all became. But what a great weekend it has been, they all agreed and said goodnight.

Sunday morning, they were driving back to Townsville in silence as each had their own thoughts about all the mysteries they had encountered at Woolgar River Park over the last four days.

Lynette was also going mentally through her list of things to buy for her new home.

Ros was thinking what lovely new friends they had met and had a great time with over the past four days and was hoping that it would become a lasting friendship.
Malcolm was thinking, "fuck work tomorrow" wishing he was retired, like Lynette and Gus.
Gus was asleep!

Lynette and Gus were back in Cairns and had both been busy shopping for the new house, it was very exciting times and the shopping list ended up being huge.

There was some consideration of whether would it be better to buy items in Townsville rather than Cairns, as Townsville was some three hundred and sixty kilometres closer to the property when travelling via the Bruce and Flinders Highways with a total trip of seven hundred and thirty kilometres.
Alternatively, there was State Route 62, which went from Cairns to Ravenshoe then Greenvale to Hughenden with a total of only five hundred and ninety kilometres, a difference

of one hundred and forty kilometres, but a shit road being about sixty per cent dirt.

They only had the one car these days, their Subaru 2.5 Outback, which was really good, but not so good when you wanted to carry heaps of stuff in it. They had decided to go the bush way on Route 62. The Subie was slowly filling up with gear and they were busy planning subtle changes to the house, which was hard as they hadn't even thought to take photos of the house when they were there. How dumb were we!!

Lynette received a phone call from Hailee, saying that a well dressed gentleman was at the property wanting to talk to her, he wanted her mobile number, should she give it to him? Lynette asked what the man wanted but Hailee said that the man would not talk to her, only Mrs Teague. "Ok," said Lynette, "give him my number and tell him to call me, I'll talk to you soon, we should be up there next Monday, did Janice get there ok, good, ok, I'll talk later, bye".

No sooner had she put down her mobile when it rang again.
"Hello," she answered.
"Mrs Teague"
"Speaking"
"It's Jason Strange, Mrs Teague, I have been having trouble contacting you, your other number has been ringing out and I have left messages"

"I'm sorry, who did you say you are" responded a confused Lynette.

The caller told her again that he was Jason Strange and that he was from Richmond Hill Real Estate at Charters Towers and he went on to say he had been trying to contact her since last Friday, as the buyer wants to do a final inspection before settlement, which is this Friday, in two days time.

Jason Strange kept on saying, "Hello,..hello Mrs Teague,... helloooo".

Lynette was totally confused and her head was spinning, what buyer, what settlement, what was happening?

She got back into the conversation and suggested "I think you may have the wrong person here, Mr Strange, I am Lynette Teague, who is it you need to talk to"

"Oh," then after a long pause, "I would like to talk to Mrs Sonia Teague, is that your mother" Strange, awkwardly replied, "It's in respect to her property 'Woolgar River Park' which we have just sold on her behalf, the settlement on the property is in two days time and the buyer has flown up from Horsham in Victoria to have another look through the property before settlement, as he is entitled. If we refuse him it could go against the sale, so it's.."

Lynette interrupted Strange, at that point and said she does not have a mother, or a mother in law called Sonia and that she and her husband were in fact the owners of 'Woolgar River Park' and that the property has not been sold, nor is it for sale.

Strange was very persistent and said that he has a binding contract signed by Lachlan and Sonia Teague.

Thinking quickly, under a mixture of confusion and hurt, not to mention shock, Lynette asked Strange for his mobile number and said that their solicitor would call him straight back.

Gus had just walked in the door at the tail end of the conversation and could see by Lynette's expression that she was deeply concerned about something.

By the time Lynette had finished telling Gus about the phone call, he too was visibly concerned and attempted to call Malcolm Davies in Townsville but his personal number and mobile number were both busy. Gus left 'urgent' messages on both telephone services, to call him back.

Lynette brought a beer out to Gus, he was sitting on the balcony staring at his mobile phone wondering what to do next. "This is fucking unreal, it can't be happening, what is going on" Gus said to no one in particular.

Gus rang Willem at the property and asked if that bloke was still there, Willem told Gus that he had left a few minutes ago, he had asked for a key to the main house, but Willem had told him he didn't have one, then he got in his car and drove off.

'Have you got the grid gate open' asked Gus, 'it is open, I haven't closed it since we got back last week with the mower, but, I was actually going to call you today about something'.

Willem went on to say that Janice had acquired a cattle dog pup in Hughenden and had brought it with her last week and that the dog had started barking last night, Tuesday night, and Willem had gone out side to see what it might be and he heard something near the Landcruiser and as he walked over in the dark, he thought he had heard someone running away.

This morning, he went to the Landcruiser to have a look around and saw that the quarter window was open on the driver's side, the side closest to the house, it had been forced open as if someone was trying to get into the Landcruiser, maybe to steal it, he had thought. So after that, he was going to lock the grid gate tonight. Gus suggested leaving it locked all the time, for the time being, and that they would see them all on Monday.

Not long after Gus had spoken to Willem, his phone rang and it was Malcolm, still on for the weekend after next, Malcolm had asked as soon as Gus answered.

Problems, Gus announced, weird problems, then he gave Malcolm the full story as he knew it.

Malcolm was also bewildered, he would give Jason Strange a call and see if he could meet him in Charters Towers later that afternoon and get a look at the sale contract and he would get back to him. Gus thanked him and asked would the sale go through, Malcolm said that he would stop the sale one way or another. He said it did not seem likely that Lachlan would set up a will and then sell the house. Anyway, even if the sale did go through then the money for the sale would belong to you Gus. I'll call you as soon as I know, probably later this evening, don't worry!

Lynette looked quizzically at Gus as he got off the mobile, Malcolm is going to see Strange, if he can this arvo in Charters Towers, to get it sorted, he said not to worry. "Not to worry, fuck me, we just don't need these sort of dramas in our life Lynette," Gus had said.

By the time Malcolm had called them at around six thirty that evening, they had both accepted that the property would most likely be sold and that it was nothing lost really, other than their time. They were still miles in front as the sales price was likely to be around the five to six million mark, which really would be better for them rather than a property.
Sadly though, in the short time they had at the property, they had both fallen in love with it.

"It's a fraud case" were Malcolm's first words, " I took a copy of Lachlan's signature from his will, the one that I witnessed and the bank details that Lachlan had submitted with me to my meeting with Strange and compared them to the details on the sales contract, total forgery of Lachlan's signature. I also had time to see the seller's conveyancing solicitor to compare signatures on the solicitors' conveyancing appointment and authority, they are totally different signatures to that of Lachlan and the bank account details for the settlement funds, totally different. So, there you go".

"I have taken all the details including copies of the contract and conveyancing authority including bank details to the Townsville police for their perusal upon my return back this evening.
So, there will be no sale" Malcolm added.

"Well, we had sort of resigned ourselves to the fact that it was probably going to be sold", said Gus over the phone to Malcolm, "I don't think you would have been too happy if that was the case old boy", said Malcolm, "the selling price was two point one million, about four and a half million short of it's estimated value. I think our Mr Strange will have a lot of explaining to do, as with some signature witness's".

"Bottom line is, the buyer will get his deposit back from the agent, the agent will have a no sale and lots of questions to answer, as with the conveyancing solicitors and of course, Mrs Sonia Teague," said Malcolm, "You two just get on with life and we will see you at Woolgar River Park on Saturday week, for the long weekend".

"We don't know how to thank you enough", said Gus on behalf of himself and Lynette," can't wait to catch up, see you then".

Lynette had made contact with an old friend at the Townsville Police Station, Detective Inspector Graham Jamison. "A blast from the past, It's been a while Gazza", Lynette said when calling the Inspector, and continued with old time memories for the next couple of minutes until she got down to business, "by any chance, are you on the Sonia Teague case," she asked.
"Never heard of it" Gazza said, "should I know about it" he asked. Lynette filled him in with all she knew about the inheritance to Gus, to the fraudulent sale of their property.
Graham Jamison sat there intrigued. "Let me make some enquiries and I will get back to you on what is happening, great talking again Linnie".

Monday morning came and the Teague's were on their way to Woolgar River Park on Route 62 with a car that was absolutely packed with pillows, enough for their bed and for a spare bed, the Davies were coming to visit next weekend, sheets, light doonas, pots, pans, cutlery, crockery, plastic storage containers, knife block with knives, knife sharpener, food stuffs as in herbs, sauces, pepper, salt, they also had some meat products and veg to get them through one night and were planning of a food shop at Richmond the next day. Most importantly was six cartons of xxxx gold stubbies packed in the back and another two cartons on ice in their huge esky.

It was around three in the afternoon when they got to the grid gate and Gus got out to unlock it, they drove through and Gus relocked the gate before driving down to the house and on onto the porte-cochere.

They had only just got out of their car when the three caretakers were there saying hello, welcome home. Gus said to all "Thirst things Thirst" and opened the back of the car to get access to the esky and pulled out five stubbies, one each for all, they all sat around the verandah drinking their beers and the caretakers telling of all the news, which was really very little other than Janice discovering a mobile telephone behind the seat of the Landcruiser. She said she would go and get it, but Gus said that it could wait till later.

Lynette told the caretakers that she had enough steak for a BBQ this evening if anyone was interested and to come down at about six. They all thought that would be magic, and said see you later as they headed back to the manager's house, about a hundred and twenty meters from the main house.

It was then into unpacking the car, but a first up job was cleaning out the fridges and freezers, all five fridges and two freezers and a cool room, and getting them going.

At around five thirty, they were somewhat set in, with their bed made and ready, no rush for the other bed as she had all week to do that, they had put the beer in the fridges, as with drinking water and Coca-Cola.

Gus turned his attention to the BBQ, it was spotless, as with everything around the house, which they now knew why, as it was on the market for sale just a little while ago.

The caretakers, or kids, as Gus had started to call them, had turned up just before six o'clock carrying drinks and chips. There was a fridge on the verandah next to the BBQ which Gus hadn't noticed until he was checking out the BBQ, it was fairly clean so he just turned it on, it now contained a carton of gold and the kids had brought a collection of cider and JB and coke with four stubbies of Great Northern.

They all sat around a huge round teak table on teak chairs with leather, or leatherish cushions on them, Janice had brought with her the mobile phone she had found in the Landcruiser, it was flat and it was an iPhone. Janice explained that none of them had an iPhone, so they had no charging cable. Gus took the iPhone inside and put it on his charging cable.

As Gus returned Janice was telling Lynette about the estate agent, Strange, Janice was saying what a creep he seemed to be, he wanted to look everywhere, and we kept telling him no. He also kept asking questions about Mrs Teague, we just assumed it was Lynette that he was talking about, "strange alright", with laughter from all.

Willem said that they had been going into Richmond for food and drinks as it was only about a forty minute drive as opposed to one and a half hours drive to Hughenden, but it wasn't as good as Hughenden, a lot smaller and a lot more expensive, but a good butcher and a supermarket and of course a pub and a bowls club.

Willem also said that he had fixed the quarter window on the cruiser, the catch was only bent, but he was certain it wasn't like that before and he was also certain that heard someone running away, and not a kangaroo.

They both woke in the morning at about the same time, and neither could believe the quiet, other than the occasional bird until a couple of kookaburras started up.

What a great bed, the mattress was unreal, they had tried to turn the mattress over before they made the bed but they hadn't been able to move it, weird but comfortable. They were sleeping in the second large bedroom, as Lynette wanted to paint the master bedroom before they moved into it. Hopefully, we can start today, thought Lynette.

Lynette said it was nine thirty, "What! You have got to be joking," said Gus and Lynette disappeared into the ensuite, Gus promptly rolled over and went back to sleep.

Gus finally got out of bed and found Lynette in the kitchen trying out one of her new frypans with some great smelling bacon, "won't be long" she said and Gus walked over to where he had the mysterious iPhone on charge and brought it back to the breakfast bar.

"Unreal, It's still connected" Gus exclaimed, "but it's locked", he wandered out to his car and brought in his laptop. The laptop showed that wifi was available but that it was locked and required a password.

Lynette brought over the breakfasts and they started to enjoy them whilst chatting about the wifi availability but wondering where it was, as neither had seen a modem, or router anywhere.

"Might be the kids?" said Gus, of course, agreed Lynette, "they would have an internet device".
"How can we unlock this phone" wondered Gus aloud, Lynette said, "There is a place in Cairns that could probably unlock it called 'King It', we should take it there next week when we are back".

Janice and Hailee arrived at the door and knocked, Gus said, "The kids I suppose" and Lynette said "that she was expecting the girls this morning for house cleaning and maybe a bit of painting, a big day" she said.

Gus said that he would go into Richmond and check out the butcher and also the price of beer at the pub. He took the Landcruiser ute.

Inside the butcher shop was a lot busier than Gus might have expected, it seemed there was about four guys working behind the counter and in the backroom. It was top looking meat, but then again, most beef seems to look good, it's not until you start to eat it that you discover whether it's good or not. Most of the beef around that area was known as Droughtmaster. One thing that Gus knew for sure was his beef.

The Droughtmaster is an Australian breed of beef cattle. It was developed from about 1915 in North Queensland by crossing Zebuine cattle with cattle of British origin, principally the Beef Shorthorn. It was the first Australian Taurindicine hybrid breed, in other words, half Brahmas and half Shorthorn, great taste but to Gus's way of thinking, tough!!

Gus asked the butcher if he had any Hereford or Lowline, a type of Angus. The butcher said he had some whole rumps of both and some whole porterhouse of Hereford.
Gus ordered two large whole rumps of the Lowline and one large of the Hereford, cut into nineteen millimetre steaks with a roast piece from each of about two kilos and a Hereford porterhouse sliced into twenty five millimetre steaks, six kilos of the beef sausages and six kilos of the thin sausages, both packed into a two kilo and a six kilo seperate pack.

The butcher issued the orders to the younger guys and told them to hop to it, he then glanced outside and said to Gus, "Are you driving Barry's ute" Gus looked to where the butcher was looking and replied, "Do you mean the white cruiser ute." "Yeah, it looks like Barry's, I'm sure". "Who is Barry," Gus wanted to know. The butcher told him that Barry was the manager at 'Woolgar Creek Park' a big cattle property just west of here, but the old bloke got crook and then sold all the cattle, so Barry ran out of a job.

The old feller kept him on though, just keeping the place neat and tidy and looking out for it.
"Where does Barry live now" asked Gus. "Barry lives out at the station with his father", the butcher said whilst packing up Gus's meat. Gus paid by EFTPOS, and two of the young fellows took the meat out to the ute. The butcher said that he hadn't seen Barry around for about a week now. Gus said thanks and drove around to the drive in bottle shop at the pub.

He drove down Harris Street and then turned into the driveway that led to the bottle shop, there was no one at the bottle shop but he could hear people in the bar, then a female voice called out, "Be right with you Barry". Gus was starting to think that Barry was a popular guy around Richmond, then again there are just under six hundred people here. A friendly lady came from the bar to the bottle shop, "Oh, it's not Barry, sorry, I thought it was someone else".

"Not a problem, good morning and can I get six cartons of xxxx Gold and three cartons of Great Northern super crisp"
"They'll have to be hot mate, I haven't got that many cold"
"That's fine, thanks" said Gus as he started to get his Nab card out to pay.
He helped the lady put the cartons in the back and held up his card as she grabbed the eftpos machine and dialled in five hundred and sixty dollars. "Having a party mate".
"No, just stocking up, got some visitors arriving soon" commented Gus.

The lady asked Gus if he lived here and Gus said, "Yes just moving in". "Well", she said," my name is Alice, and I always welcome thirsty new customers, where about are you living" she asked.

Gus introduced himself and said he was living at his uncle's place thirty odd kilometres along the river road. Alice was on the ball as she said, "Ah, Lachie's place, that's why you're driving Barry's ute". Gus said, "Yes it is Lachlan's place he was moving into, and yes it was Barry's ute and to save answering too many questions also added that he had to get back soon".
But Alice wanted a conversation. "Sad about Lachie, such a great bloke, you must get on well with Sonia, if you are living there".
Gus did not want to get into a conversation about anyone from the property at this stage and told Alice that he would

have to catch up with her later and repeated that he had to get back.

Gus was thinking on the way back, that it was all getting stranger, what with Barry being pretty well known and people assuming that he still lived at the property, and..with his father?

Gus stopped the cruiser at the manager's house and got one of the lowline beef rump packs and the two kilo pack of sausages from the floor of the passengers side and took them up to the front verandah where Willem was just coming out of the front door.

Gus handed the meat to Willem and said there is a carton of Great Northern for you too, Willem took the meat and placed it on a table just inside the entry and came out for the beer asking how much did he owe Gus. "Nothing," said Gus, "just a little thank you gift, I won't make it a habit though, I promise you".

Back at the main house and placing the meat into the fridges for sorting out a bit later, then as much beer as he could load into the fridges and the balance into the cool room, he took a cold stubbie from the fridge and sat out on the front verandah in the shade.

It wasn't long until Lynette found him out there and went and got two more stubbies and brought them to where he was sitting. Gus said to her "Cheers! What's new"? Lynette said "Heaps what's new with you", Gus repeated Lynette's comment questioningly "Heaps, such as...what."

"Well", said Lynette, "we were up there in the master bedroom, as you know, to get the walls ready for painting, which incidentally, has had the second coat and looks great, but as Hailee was removing the left hand side drapes from the window on the right side of the bed, we all heard something fall on the floor. It sounded like a five cent piece or something like that and Janice called out and said, "Look it's a bullet". I went over just as she was about to pick it up, and told her not to touch it. It was a spent cartridge case, a twenty two. I went down to the kitchen and got a small freezer bag and a toothpick and went back and picked it up with the toothpick and placed it into the freezer bag.

"Gus", Lynette suddenly looked very serious, "I think that bedroom may be a murder scene".
"No way", said Gus, but Lynette cut him off. "Why would a twenty two case be stuck in the drapes Gus! Think about it". We had almost finished doing the whole wall behind the bed and around the other window on the right side of the bed, so I didn't see any sense in stopping now, as if there was any other evidence then we had already destroyed it. But I really think it is very suspicious!!

After they had discovered the spent case that morning, Lynette had both Hailee and Janice write and sign a statuary declaration with respect to the discovery of the cartridge case and also their opinion that it was dislodged from the left hand side window drape. That is how important I think it is Gus.

It was Gus that got up from his chair on the verandah this time, to get two more beers, he returned and said that he was still not quite with it, why Lynette thought that this twenty two case was so important.

"Okay", consider this Gus, "if I was to fire a rifle through that bedroom window, if it was an automatic rifle it would eject the case to the right, if it was a manual rifle and I worked the bolt, it would also eject to the right. This case was dislodged from the left hand side drapes of the right hand side window, not the right hand side drapes, are you starting to get the picture, Gus"?
"Not really, are you suggesting that someone fired a rifle into the wall to the left side of the window"? "No Gus, not really, as a rifle barrel even hard up against the wall, when the case was ejected it would most probably be well away from the window drapes and the case would most likely end up on the bed". Well, you have certainly lost me this time Lynette, Gus mused.

"Gus, what I am suggesting, is that someone has shot an automatic pistol into the bed very close to the wall, the spent case would then eject from the right hand side of the automatic handgun and could possibly lodge in the drapes".

Gus looked stupefied, "and are there any holes in the mattress Lynette", Gus said sarcastically.

"No Gus, there are no holes in the mattress", Lynette quipped, starting to get annoyed at the stupidity that Gus can display sometimes. Lynette got up and went into the kitchen and brought back her hard covered notebook that she had used for the girl's declarations, she sat at the table on the verandah and drew a picture for Gus.

Gus looked at the finished picture, it was an aerial view of, he guessed the master bedroom, it showed the bed in between two windows, it showed a person lying on the right hand side of the bed.

It showed another person standing next to the prone person with a gun in his/her hand and a line displaying a possible trajectory of a spent case into the left hand drapes of the right hand window.

Gus's mouth dropped open. "What, what the fuck…are you suggesting….fuck me,..no way".

Lynette invited Gus to come up with another scenario, other than someone, either throwing a spent cartridge case at the drapes or placing a case inside the heavy folds of the drapes, doubtful, Lynette added.

There were no cold beers left in the fridge on the verandah, Lynette went inside to the fridge in the kitchen while Gus filled the verandah fridge with more from the cool room to the bar.

Lynette said that they really needed to know where Lachlan had died and what had caused his death and had there been an autopsy. Gus suggested that maybe they should call the police, Lynette said that they would most probably laugh at us, she was remembering cases back in her police days when they would suggest that people watched too much TV.

Lynette confided in Gus that she had already been in contact with Graham Jamison at the Townsville police station with respect to Sonia and her fraudulent activities and she might also tell Graham about the spent twenty two cartridge case and mention her theory to him, as he could get the answers on Lachlans cause of death and location. "Too late for today", Lynette said, "I'll give him a hoy tomorrow. What do you want for dinner Gus, did you get some steak from Richmond"?

"I certainly did, two lots to choose from, Lowline, or Hereford". Lynette said she'd go the Aberdeen, she also being a beef connoisseur, knew exactly what a Lowline referred to when it came to beef.

From one slice of the rump beef, Gus cut and trimmed two good looking steaks, salted them on both sides and let them acquire room temperature for about an hour before adding a little Avocado oil and black pepper, then cooking in one of Lynette's new Tefal Skillets at a hot temperature then using a little more Avocado oil to seal each side, heat down a little and turn the steaks and then a dash of Hanford Port to finish them off. They were served with, slowly cooked in just boiling water, chat potatoes doused in butter together with fresh (ish) green beans. No wine with this meal, just beer, delicious!

What a very busy Monday, Gus had not even had time to tell Lynette about Richmond and Barry.

Who is Barry

Neither of them had slept very well that night, regardless of the large quantity of stubbies they had consumed. Tuesday, the girls had arrived at about eight thirty, eager to get into the master bedroom. Lynette and Gus were having a light breakfast in the kitchen when Gus had told her about his trip to Richmond yesterday and more to the point about Barry.

He told her that the butcher had asked him if that was Barry's ute he was driving and had told Gus that Barry and his father, both lived at Woolgar River Park. The woman at the bottle shop had also assumed it was Barry driving the ute, and when Gus had told her that we had moved into Woolgar River Park, she assumed also that we got on well with Sonia.

They both agreed that they should spend a bit of time at the pub in Richmond as they may learn more about Barry and his father.

Lynette had a great conversation with Graham Jamison at Townsville police station, he had told her that Sonia Teague had in fact engaged Jason Strange of Richmond Hill Real Estate at Charters Towers to sell the property Woolgar River Station for two point one million dollars.

Apparently, Strange had suggested that as a ridiculous price and that a figure of around four million dollars would perhaps be more appropriate and suggested that a valuation should be sought prior to exposing the property to the market. Mrs Teague apparently would hear none of that and insisted on her price for a quick sale as Mr Teague's health was in rapid decline.

"But", said Lynette, "Lachlan Teague's signature that was on the contract to sell was a fake". "Yes it seems it was, but according to Strange, Lachlan was present when Strange went to the property for a look around and obtained Lachlan's signature on the sales engagement form", said Graham Jamison. "When the property was snapped up by the Horsham buyer, again Strange visited the property with the contract of sale and again received Teague's signature".
It was just becoming more confusing to everyone.

"And what's more", said Graham, "We can't find Sonia Teague and no one seems to know where she is, I have to go now, I will keep you posted", Graham was about to hang up when Lynette told him of the spent cartridge. Graham had listened intently, he found it most plausible, as it had come from a former detective sergeant with a very high rating reputation. Graham said he would get more information and also that he would like to view this particular room if that was possible.
Lynette suggested that he should come out to the property and bring his wife Stefanie next weekend, as it is a long weekend and their solicitor, who is also a friend will be

there. "Sounds good" Graham had said, book us in, we'll be there on Friday afternoon.

Lynette briefed Gus on the conversation with Graham Jamison, Gus said the only bit of proof on our side with the sale is the different signatures, it seems.

As she was telling Gus about Graham and Stefanie coming out this weekend, she suddenly realised she did not have any sheets, pillows or a doona for a third bed, and she would need more towels, she said: "shit, we have no queen size bedding, Charters Towers is probably the closest and that is over four hundred hundred kilometres from here, Fuck It"!

Gus suggested she give Ros a call and ask her if she can buy the bedding items for you and she can get the store to call you for your credit card details for payment. "Brilliant," said Lynette as she started to dial Ros's number.

"When you're done there, how about we head into Richmond, I want to see the local stock and station agent about cattle agistment and we can check out the Palace Hotel", Gus said heading out the door to get the Subie.

The Subaru certainly handled the dirt roads better than the Landcruiser ute as far as creature comfort, they stopped at the stock agents in Goldring Street, just two doors up from the pub.

The lady at the agents sang out a cheery good morning, followed by oh sorry, it's afternoon, but only just, so I am forgiven and what can I do for you?

We would like to talk to someone in relation to cattle agistment if we could replied Gus. The lady told them that Peter was away just now, but expected back in about half an hour, if you'll leave your name and contact number, I'll get him to call you.

Sounds good, It's Gus and Lynette, best number would be my mobile number. She wrote down the number and said he'll be onto it as soon as he gets back.

They then walked toward the pub for lunch, drinks and maybe some more info about Barry.

Lynette asked Gus why he hadn't given the lady at the stock agents their surname as well as their Christian names. Gus told her that he wasn't in the mood for too many questions just yet.

Lynette walked to the bar as Gus went to the gents, and Alice at the bar asked her what she would like. Lynette told her, two stubbies of gold and a lunch menu, please.

Alice was just serving the drinks when Gus returned to the bar, Alice said "Gus, isn't it, you were here yesterday". "You have that right Alice, this is my wife Lynette". Alice looked towards Lynette and said "Pleased to meet you Lynette, I'm Alice", "And you too" replied Lynette.

They ordered the 'T' bone steak, chips and salad and two more golds. Alice said it was a good choice as she walked through to the kitchen, she then got the beers and asked was that cash or EFTPOS, Lynette held up her card and Alice held the EFTPOS machine under it.

Alice said to Lynette, "How are you getting on with Sonia"

"Hmmm, Sonia Teague," asked Lynette.

"Sonia Teague, is it now? The last time I saw her it was still Harris" Alice spat back, as she went to the kitchen in response to the bell and came back with the two meals.

There was no one else sitting at the bar so they thought they might as well eat their meals there whilst chatting to Alice, who seemed to be quite happy talking about Sonia, whom evidently, from Alice's tone, she did not have much time for.

"Did that bitch tell you she was married to Lachie, that'd be a laugh, poor old Lachie, god bless his soul" Alice said vehemently, "Lachie wouldn't have had her there except she was good at cooking and cleaning. Didn't you know Lachie was the other way"?

"The other way" came from Lynette, "what other w a…..y, oh, do you mean."

"Yeah", said Alice, "I think most people around here think that. Don't get me wrong people, Lachie was the best, he was always pleasant, kind and helpful to anyone who needed help. And it didn't worry me in the slightest that he was queer, or gay, as they call them now."

"Another two stubbies", Alice asked picking up the empty stubbies.

"Yes, thanks Alice" Gus spoke, feeling a bit shocked, to say the least. That little bit of info from Alice, said in one sentence had just blown them both away.

"So, Sonia was the housekeeper" suggested Gus, but other people were starting to come into the bar and it was getting hard to continue the conversation with Alice. They drank their beers and left the pub to go back to the stock agent's office.

Just as they were approaching the stock agent's door, Gus's phone rang, "Hello, this is Gus."
It was the stock agent, who quickly realised and put down his phone and called out, "Gus and Lynette" as they walked through the door. They all grinned and introduced each other, this time Gus mentioned their surname, Teague. Any relation to Lachlan Teague the agent had asked and Gus told him that he was his late uncle and that he and Lynette had decided to stay on for a while at the property and see what transpires. Hence their visit today.

The stock agent, Peter Lansky, had known Lachlan quite well and had done business with him often during the past seven or so years that he had been there. He was mainly buying and selling cattle and he asked if Gus was in the market for yearlings. Gus and Lynette were not in the financial position to purchase.

Gus mentioned he was interested in agisting out the land and what were Peter's thoughts. Peter told him they were very good just now and his location was good as they could get road trains into there but the area did not demand big agistment fees. Peter Lansky, knew Woolgar River Park and had thought that around the five thousand head would be a good number for the property as it had very good water and is well grassed with Buffel Grass, Curly Mitchell, Flinders Grass, Forest Mitchell, Seca Stylo and the property has been seeded with various Buffel varieties. The fencing was in good order the last time he looked.

He added that Barry and his team are pretty well on the ball with fencing repairs and pump maintenance. Probably looking at between three dollars and four fifty, depending on present conditions around the property. He said he would need to go out to the property though to better assess the situation for agistment. They thanked him and said they would be in touch later this week.

In the car heading back to their homestead, Lynette asked what did the three dollars and four fifty mean. Gus told her that he did not have a clue, but did not want to show his ignorance, he would google it up once he got back. She reminded him about the internet at Woolgar River Park, and he replied "shit yeah, we've got to find that fucking internet." "And", said Lynette, "how about this fucking Sonia!, and what do think of your uncle being gay".

Gus just grinned and shook his head, "The plot thickens, I can't wait for Malcolm and Graham to get up here, what a discussion we're going to have". "Yes" agreed Lynette, "and we also need to find out more about Barry, we might need him for the cattle agistment thing".

It was still pretty early afternoon when they arrived back, and Gus was determined to sort out this internet issue. Their iPhones and iPads and Gus's Mac AirBook laptop all showed a strong wifi signal around the house which diminished when moving away from the house, so the internet modem/router was somewhere in the house.

They needed to find this modem to obtain the password from it so they could join this wifi service.

They could see the internet antenna on the roof, so maybe the only way was to follow where the cable went. There were two Mac desktop PCs in the house but they both wanted passwords, so they were of no use.

He spoke to Willem and asked what he knew about the internet. Willem said he had also found that there was wifi available and was going to ask Gus for the password so that he could use it. Gus gave him the heads up about the wifi situation and they both went to look at the roof, then inside the house upstairs looking for an access panel, which they found on the small landing on the rear staircase that leads to the laundry.

Gus asked Willem if he had seen any step ladders or such around anywhere and Willem said he hadn't so Gus sent him off in the ute to go get a two point four metre, aluminium step ladder from the Hardware store in Richmond and told him to get the store to ring him for card details.

Gus went down to the verandah that he had now nicknamed the 'beer garden' and took a stubbie from the fridge. It wasn't long before Lynette in company with Hailee and Janice also arrived at the beer garden, "I'm shouting the girls a drink, they have done a wonderful job on the master bedroom, we can probably move into it tomorrow and they can start on the other King room and one of the queen rooms and have them ready by Friday, just in time for the visitors".

Willem arrived as we were all on our third, or fourth beer, he was carrying the ladder and asked Gus where did he want it. Gus told him it could wait till tomorrow, "Here Willem have a beer".

Gus asked him why the hardware store didn't call him for payment, Willem replied that they said they have opened an account for us, as they knew who Gus was.

Small towns, Gus contemplated, two visits to town and everyone now knows who he is, and he supposed, what he was doing. Ahh well, happy days.

While chatting and drinking, Gus had mentioned the two Mac desktops and Hailee said she might be able to reset and reload the MacOS on them. She then said she used to work for an IT company in London, specialising in Macs. Gus just shook his head, he had never even thought to ask these guys what they were all about. "For fucks sake," Gus said, more to himself.

Lynette interrupted and reminded Hailee that they were painting tomorrow, not playing with computers. Hailee laughed and said she would take one to their house with her to do it at night, it would be easier that way.

The next morning, at about eight thirty, the girls were there ready for work. Willem had gone back to the hardware store in Richmond for more roller covers and paint, and this and that, what Lynette had wanted. Hailee was carrying a Mac desktop, Gus had forgotten that she had taken it with her yesterday afternoon, she simply said it's all good and connected to the wifi, I can't get the wifi password from it though, so you will still have to find the modem. But, she went on, it's as good as gold, very quick. "It's had its hard drive contents erased by someone who must know just enough to be dangerous" Hailee giggled, "they didn't empty the trash can".

She told Gus, that happened quite a lot with people who did not understand the MacIntosh operating systems correctly, so this one is full of shit." What sort of shit do you mean Hailee," Gus asked inquisitively. "Just files and stuff, you know, banking, stock valuations, all that type of shit and some of it is protected".

Great, Gus thought as he googled about cattle agistment and found the rates to be weekly. At his quick calculation, five thousand head at four dollars equalled around just over one million dollars per year. Good money if they could get that much, it was of course less the costs of the staff required to look after them, fencing repairs, bore fuel and repairs, and so on and so on, but just rough figures look good. Just depends on how many cattle we can find to agist, Gus was thinking.

It was Friday morning, the girls had finished painting the super king bedroom, the king and one queen bedroom. The drapes and curtains in the rooms had been cleaned and the rooms looked great. There was no bedding yet to put into the queen room, but that was arriving by Ros, hopefully, this weekend. Gus and Lynette had moved into the super king, or master bedroom and everything was just falling nicely into place.

Lynette was looking forward to the visitors that would be arriving today from Townsville, new friends Malcolm and Ros, she was putting into the king room and Graham and Stefanie into a queen room, so nice to have all these rooms when having people stay.

Gus had prepared three porterhouse steaks cut in half and trimmed of excess fat to make six three hundred gram steaks, they were salted and seasoned and placed in the fridge. He also made a spicy, peppered potato's and cheese casserole, to be served with mushrooms.
He had then taken two cartons of gold and one carton of super crisp from the cool room and placed them into the fridge on the verandah and into the bar fridge. Lynette had

just arrived back from Richmond with two bottles of Paringa Estate Riesling, that's all Alice had and a carton of Jacobs Creek classic sauvignon blanc. She had also bought two bottles of Johny Walker black label. She had also picked up two kilos of mushrooms for dinner that night.

Malcolm and Ros had arrived at four thirty that afternoon, after leaving Townsville at eleven o'clock that morning. Ros had brought with her the four pillows, pillowcases, two sets of four hundred count sheet sets in pale pastel grey and a doona with a dark grey cover and a dark grey bathroom set. I do hope the colours are what you wanted Ros asked Lynette, she had tried to follow Lynette's colour request. Lynette and Ros took the linen and doona up to the queen room that had been painted. Ros could not believe the difference that the paint had made to the rooms. They finished making up the queen room and went down to find the men in the bar with drinks happening."Beer Ros, or something different" asked Lynette as she opened the bar fridge and getting two more gold stubbies for Malcolm and Gus. Ros also had a stubbie, so as not to get too tipsy before the other guests, whom Lynette had told her all about, whilst making the bed, had arrived. Graham and Stefanie arrived just as it was getting dark.

Lynette introduced Graham and Stefanie to Malcolm and Ros then asked Gus if he remembered them which of course he said he did, trying to think hard then it came to him, the wedding.

"Looking good Gus", Graham said while extending his hand to Gus, Stefanie also said hello it's good to see you both, nice to meet you, you too, haven't changed, you neither, how long has it been? All that done and over with, into the bar for a drink, which extended to three drinks and then onto the verandah for dinner, as it was getting on to seven o 'clock by this stage.

Lynette took Graham and Stefanie on a house tour whilst Gus got dinner ready, the talk over dinner was a bit subdued as the visitors were all visibly worn out and tired from the over five hundred kilometre journey that afternoon. They only touched briefly on the fraudulent activities and associated mysteries and all decided to leave that discussion for tomorrow.
It was an early night for everyone, except Gus and Graham who decided to stay up until around two am, playing pool and drinking beers.

Ros and Lynette had prepared breakfast on the verandah the next morning during which Malcolm had produced the topographical map which included Woolgar River Park, that he had brought with him. Indicating to the map, he suggested they all go for a drive of discovery around the property as there seemed to be some interesting places to look at such as a gorge in the river, some buildings in the centre of the property and also the other house on the property.

Malcolm's VX Landcruiser was a seven seat so it was the obvious choice, Gus's large portable esky was filled with as much ice as they could find around the house and then drinks were added.

Great sightseeing was enjoyed and all were quite amazed at the vast area of the property. They found what was left of a six stand shearing shed, shearer's quarters and cookhouse, indicating that this was once a sheep property. Driving on they finally reached the far boundary after about twenty seven kilometres, then driving to the left, they drove for a further thirteen kilometres to the northern boundary, then turned south in the direction of the homestead.

It was about another twenty kilometres towards the homestead they came across the fourth residence on the property. As they approached the house everyone looked in shock to see somebody sitting on the verandah, and even waved as they got closer, then got from their chair and walked to the edge of the verandah as Malcolm stopped at the front of the house.

They all alighted from the Landcruiser and walked towards the person on the verandah who now shouted out to them "Good Day all, I suppose I had better put the kettle on"

As they walked to the entrance it was visible to see that whoever this person was, seemed to be a long time resident.

"Angus Teague, I presume" said the man, with his arm outstretched heading towards Gus and introducing himself "Owen Harrigan". Gus acknowledged Owen and shook his hand.

"Tea, anyone" Owen called out, "please come on up and take a seat here at the table"

All declined the offer of tea, but Gus suggested a cold beer, to which Owen said that he could not help them there. Malcolm, already on his way to the cruiser to get the drinks, asked "Will you have a beer Owen"? Owen responded with a "love one thank you", and reminded everyone to have a seat.

Gus sat down next to Owen and asked him if he should know him, as he was living in Gus's house.

Owen said that he had been intending on coming up to the homestead and introducing himself, but he thought that he would let Gus settle in a bit first.

Owen, went on to explain that he had been on Woolgar River Park for nearly thirty years, as the station manager and with two different owners, and that his son Barry had recently taken over from him because he was getting a little long in the tooth.

Gus was thinking that this is just what he needs, someone who can tell him the history of this place."Owen, how about coming down up to the homestead for dinner tonight and you can tell me, well, you can tell all of us about the history of Woolgar River Park" Gus announced.

Lynette had prepared two, two kilogram roast rump pieces in two camp ovens that she had found around the homes at the property. There was an old existing fireplace at the back of the cool room that she had got Willem to clean out and provide firewood for it, and there she cooked the two roast rumps. She prepared roast potatoes and pumpkin in the kitchen oven and microwaved Brussels sprouts and green peas.

Owen Harrigan had arrived in his 1949 Landrover Series 1 with a bottle of Chivas Regal. You could hear him coming from some distance, you could hear more the transmission than the motor, everyone walked to the porte-cochere, not to welcome him, but really just to look at what the noise was. It was a splendid original example and looked to have been really well looked after. Owen said it was all he had since his son Barry had borrowed his other car. They all went into the bar for a drink.

This was to be the first time they were using the dining area, it contained a beautiful table with six legs crafted from Australian Corymbia maculata, more commonly known as spotted gum, as with the tabletop.
Many items in the home were crafted from this particular timber, including all the floor timbers. The table had ten chairs and set out as four on each side and one on each end. For tonight Lynette had set three on each side and one on the end.

Both of the roasts were partly sliced, and placed on a large stainless steel serving tray then placed on the large matching dining buffet, that was placed in front of the dining table and separated by about two and a half metres. The roast potatoes were served on two separate trays, and the pumpkin Brussels sprouts and peas on a single serving platter with two gravy boats, each placed on either side. It looked impressive and very inviting.

There were no arguments about the quality of the meal and not much of the beef left or anything left of the accompaniments. Owen, sitting at the head of the table and sipping a wine declared it the best meal he had in years, all agreed and the table was cleared of the plates and cutlery and replaced with more wine bottles and Owen's bottle of Chivas Regal. Gus found some glasses of odd shapes and sizes behind the bar and Graham put together a bucket of ice, Ros found two more bottles of sauv blanc and all were brought to the dining table. Gus made sure everyone had drinks then asked Owen when he had first arrived at Woolgar River Park.

Do you know it was once called 'Woolgar River Curse' by the locals around Richmond for a while? Everyone went silent and just looked at Owen as if he had shot a gun.

Owen had arrived in Richmond as the new bank manager for the ES&A Banking Co. at the grand age of forty. He had been working as an accountant with Esanda in Brisbane and he had scored a promotion as a Bank Manager, promotion my arse, he told everyone, no other prick wanted to leave Brissy to come out here to woop woop, that is except muggins here, who happened to think it might be quite an adventure. Owen's wife Jenny was also keen to get out of Brisbane.

Owens's son, Barry was nineteen years old and was just finishing his apprenticeship as a mechanic, he only had three months to go until completion and had stayed back in Brisbane with his employer and would come out to Richmond when finished.

Whilst working in the bank in Brisbane, Owen went on, if you looked out of the seventh floor window, where he worked, you could only see other buildings across from you, it was a much better view inside looking at the walls. But in Richmond, when he looked out of the window from his office, he saw sunshine, hills, people walking around in shorts and navy blue singlets and here he was, stuck inside the bank. A fellow called Curtis Southwell, came into the bank from time to time, generally to withdraw a bit of money from time to time. I didn't really get to meet him or to get to know him. But one day I went for Lunch at the Palace and I had a feed there and a couple of beers. I started talking to the blokes in the bar and had a few more beers and I never went back to the bank. They gave me the arse of course, and I couldn't care less, they gave me a month to get out of the bank's house. I didn't know what I was going to do, but I wasn't going back to the city.

We had only been there not quite three months and Barry was due to arrive in town pretty soon, but there seemed to be plenty of workaround for mechanics, not so for bank managers though.

About a week after I'd left the bank I was back in the pub having a drink when this fellow Curtis Southwell came up to me and says, "How are you doin Owen, I'll buy you a beer, have a seat".

The Curse

Curtis said to Owen, "Hear you've left the bank Owen", it was more of a statement, and Owen had responded that the bank had not really been for him. Curtis reminded him that there were not many office jobs around Richmond for bankers. After the next beer, Owen had told Curtis that he was finished with banks and that he wanted to do something outdoors. Curtis came straight out with it and said he had a job for Owen on his station if he wanted it and Owen just automatically said, "What doing Curtis?". Curtis replied, "The Station Manager of Woolgar River Park, is the job if you want it".

Owen then told Curtis that he had no experience whatsoever in cattle, sheep, horses or even dogs and chooks, cause I've lived all my life in Brisbane.
Cutis Southwell advised Owen that he did not need to know anything about animals, as they employed other people to look after animals, it was a Manager he was looking for, not a farm labourer. Now listen carefully Owen, because I don't stuff around and I don't want other people to stuff me around. This is how much I will pay you each month, I will also give you a two bedroom house and meat, you can also have a ute that I have there, but you will need to stay there for at least twelve months. Can you do that? Do you want the

job?, if you do, then your on as from now, otherwise I will just walk away.

Everyone at the table was intently looking and listening to Owen, he had them captured and as he raised his glass to drink his final dregs, Graham jumped up from the table and brought more drinks to the table as Malcolm poured more ice and Chivas regal into Owen's glass.

"Well you know", continued Owen, "I fucking nearly choked to death on my beer, whilst trying to say fucking, yes, yes, yes". The table erupted in laughter as Owen went on. "Sorry ladies"!
And it happened, then and there, Owen left the pub with Curtis and they drove to Woolgar River Park. Curtis showed Owen the two bedroom home, the one behind the present Manager's house. Owen added, and he showed him the old Landrover series one and said to him to use it to move your stuff out from Richmond, come and see me when you are settled. And, that is how I became the Manager of this place, finished Owen.

Curtis Southwell was around the fifty mark when Owen had met up with him. He had a lovely wife Peggy, and two sons Kevin, twenty five and Dillon, 23. They also had a daughter Cathy aged 20.
They had owned Woolgar River Park since Curtis's father had died.

"But, what's with the curse"? Ros asked. "How much time, more importantly, how much grog have we got," said Owen, causing even more laughter. More drinks all round.
Well, we both, Jenny and myself loved it here. Jenny took it upon herself to look after the chooks, not just with feeding and egg collecting, but also with breeding them for table meat.
Barry arrived and Curtis instantly proclaimed him to be the Stations Mechanic and gave him a wage.

The property was doing okay but Owen found quite a few ways of saving substantial amounts of money and Curtis implemented them. Curtis had been contemplating building a new house for quite some time, and as things were going quite well, he engaged an Architect from Mount Isa, together with a builder from Mount Isa and created the dream home they wanted with a bedroom for each of the kids and a guest bedroom, not to mention their own huge bedroom and all the other trimmings that you see here today.

Well, they moved into the new house and we moved into the old house and everything was great.
The three boys got on well together but Owen's son, Barry was always trying to "root" Cathy, who got fed up of it and told her father, who put the ultimatum to Owen that the boy had to go, or that they all go. Sorry, Owen he had said, but he could not handle it otherwise. So Barry got a job in town and found accommodation there also.

Just after that, Kevin and Dillon were out one night spotlight shooting and called into the other house, where I am living now, explained Owen. There used to be an Aboriginal stockman named Kurrie, that lived there with his wife and daughter of around sixteen, or seventeen. The boys always took cans of beer with them when they went shooting, not safe I know, Owen had added.

Well, this night they had caught a couple of nice little sucker pigs and had called in to drop the off the pigs off for Kurrie who used to raise them on wheat and corn for pork.

Anyway, Kurrie was away somewhere or other, and the boys put the pigs in Kurrie's pen and then had a beer, and Kurrie's wife had some beer with them, and the things got out of hand with the young blokes and you can image the rest of it. I won't go into detail said Owen.

Well a couple of days later and Kurrie gets back home and the wife tells Kurrie about Mr Southwell's boys.

So the next morning, quite early, there was a bashing at Curtis's door, it kept going on and on, so I gets up to see what going on, just as Curtis opens his front door. Well, here is Kurrie with only a pair of jocks on, and he's got white paint splattered all over him and he has two spears in his hand. Kurrie is jumping up and down and keeps pointing the two spears at Curtis who is telling him to fuck off.

Owen went over to help Curtis, Kurrie is yelling at Curtis demanding his boys be brought out so that Kurrie can spear them.

After a while and a lot of talking, both Curtis and Owen get the gist that the boys got Kurrie's wife pissed and then fucked his daughter. Nasty business said Curtis and he will punish his boys, not Kurrie!

Anyway, Curtis finally gets it through to Kurrie to go away and that he will not be spearing his sons and that he can pack up and fuck off.
Kurrie really had the shits bad, so he puts a curse on Curtis and his family plus the whole property, and it took a while really, with his dancing and pointing his spears to the sky, then at Curtis, then the house, then at the ground and lots of jumping and wailing.

In the end, Curtis goes inside his house and came back with a side by side twelve gauge and tells Kurrie to get off the property now. So, Kurrie went, still cursing, mind you.

That seemed to be the end of that, and Curtis told his kids to behave, or something like that. The boys were both in their mid twenty's, bit hard to reprimand at that age, but, interestingly, the boys neither came out to help their father when Kurrie was carrying on.

It was probably only about a week after the Kurrie episode, that Cathy was out riding her horse and she did not return, just her horse. We were all out in the dark looking for her, Me, Jenny, Peggy, Kevin, Dillon and Curtis. It was Curtis who found her in the river with her head split open.
The police were called out and decided, then and there, that she had been thrown from her horse.

Curtis was pretty upset as you can imagine, but he was back to the scene at the river the next morning, just looking and looking, he was getting madder the longer he looked.

He went to the coppers that morning in Richmond and told them they were all fucking idiots and to get their arses out to the river so they can see it was a murder and arrest that bastard Kurrie. Curtis said he knew Kurrie was responsible for it and he was going to get the prick if the coppers didn't. He was talking about killing Kurrie and the police told him to calm down or he would find himself locked up.

Curtis finally did calm down some but was certainly intent on getting revenge on Kurrie, who seemed to have disappeared with his family

The funeral happened, it was really sad, Barry went to the funeral but when Curtis saw him he went off his head big time and told Barry to get away from his daughter and the funeral, in no uncertain terms. I felt sorry for Curtis, but that was no way to treat Barry. I felt sorry for Barry too.

The Johnny Walker had to be opened as the Chivas was gone, and more wine came to the table as did stubbies of beer. It gets worse said Owen, as everyone sat down in silence.

Would not have been a month after Cathy's funeral, the the two boys were on their quaddies up at the top doing some fencing, they originally had Yamaha Grizzly 250's but they told their old man that they were useless as they could not carry enough tools and gear on them and what they really needed was 500 Grizzly's. There was nothing wrong with the 250's, they were great bikes. I've still got one, added Owen, they wanted the bigger bikes so they could go quicker, that's all.

Well, no one knows what happened, but the boys never came back from fencing that night. It wasn't till around two o'clock in the morning that the parents started to wonder. It was not unusual for them not to come home until daylight, but they were worried.
Curtis got his cruiser out at about three o'clock that morning and headed to where he thought the boys had been working that day.

He only got about seven kilometres up the track, just near where the hills get a bit steep when going around the steep corner, something in the middle of the track caused him to brake and swerve so suddenly to the left, that his Landcruiser went off the track and down the embankment.

Peggy was knocking, actually, banging on our door at around four o'clock that morning screaming that something was wrong. It took her a while until she was able to tell us the story and then it did not really make sense, but we got the gist of it and I told Jenny to call the police and then take care of Peggy. I went out and got into the Landrover and headed up to the top.

I had no idea where the boys had been working on the fences so he tried to follow Curtis's cruiser tracks. Where the roads intersect with three turnoffs, I connected my spotlight to the Landrover's internal plug and held it out of the window to find the tracks to follow.

When I found Curtis's tracks it was now pretty easy to follow and hopefully, I would find Curtis.

Just as I got onto the bendy bit of track I saw a reflection to my left, down the bank towards the river. I stopped the Landrover and swung the spotlight towards where I had thought I saw the reflection and instantly I could see that the reflection was the rear lights of Curtis's Landcruiser, it was upside down.

I had never even thought to bring a torch and it was dangerous to try to walk down the embankment in the dark. I was thinking how dumb was I for not having a torch in the car.

I tried to set the spotlight up so it would give me some light so that I could get down to the cruiser, but it was just out of range for the spotlight, it must have been a bit more than a hundred, maybe a hundred and fifty metres. It's hard to guess in the dark and it was dark.

Owen went on, I got down there after falling a couple of times and I could see nothing, I couldn't hear anything other than my Landrover idling away, I had to leave it running to keep the spotlight working, or it would have gone flat.

I called out to Curtis a couple of times but I couldn't hear anything except for the bloody Landrover, I felt around a bit and put my hand into something that felt like blood as it was a warm, sticky feeling, but thankfully it turned out to be oil. I called out a few more times and then thought that this was no good, even if I found him I could not do anything in the dark, so I stumbled back heading towards the spotlight which was worse than when coming down.

I had to turn the Landrover around to get back to the station and I knew that going forward there was nowhere to turn around safely in the dark, so I reversed to where I thought it was safe, turned around and got back as fast as I could.

Jenny and Peggy came running out of the house before I had stopped the Landrover and I ran past them to get to the phone. Peggy was screaming "What's wrong, what's wrong" but I just had to ignore her and I rang Triple Zero cos I knew they wouldn't answer the phone at Richmond and anyway I didn't know the number.

The operator just kept asking question after question, and I just kept saying Ambulance, Ambulance, and I gave her our location about ten times. It was about five o'clock and just starting to get light and no one had arrived. Both Peggy and Jenny were hysterical, so I said wait here and I will go back up now it's getting light. They both grabbed at me and said no stay here, don't leave us. Just as I was about to go we heard the helicopter and saw its spotlight panning around for somewhere to land. As they landed I raced up to them and shouted out that the accident was about eight kilometres to the north, the loadmaster told me to get in and show them.

It took no time for the helicopter to get to where the Landcruiser was laying upside down, but, what caught everyone's eye, was the two quad bikes smashed together head on, just a little further up the track.
The helicopter had to land further back down on the track near where I had turned the landrover around and I and the two paramedics ran up the track towards the, well now, two accidents.
In the daylight, it was easier to see the quaddies on the track before the landcruiser down the embankment.

Approaching the quaddies, the body of one of the boys could be seen just to the right of the smash.
As we got to the quaddies, the other boy's body could be seen down the embankment just up from the Landcruiser.

One Paramedic went directly down to the body at the embankment and the other went to the body on the track. The Paramedic on the track quickly turned to the other Paramedic who had already reached the body down on the embankment as was heading to the Landcruiser, he shouted out to him that he would call back up.
Owen stopped talking as his eyes were welling with tears.
Ros started to clear wine bottles from the table and Lynette

went for more drinks. The other three men were just sitting there at the table in disbelief.

Owen excused himself and went to the toilet, he didn't need directions, he knew this place like his own home. They had all settled back down at the table, kindly refusing Lynette's invitation to sit on the lounge. They all looked towards Owen and Stefanie asked if they were all dead.

"Yes, all three, father and his two sons, tragic", answered Owen.

Owen continued, Poor Mrs Southwell, Peggy just could not handle it and suffered a heart attack when she was told that all of her family had been killed. Ironically, it was the very helicopter that had been called out for her husband that had taken her to the Mount Isa hospital where she later died. They were now all totally stunned, "Wow", said Lynette, "We had no idea of such a tragedy". "Well, it was a long time ago" offered Owen, "It'd be going on seventeen years just now, it was on the National News and in all the Newspapers about the accidents on Woolgar River Station". It certainly put Richmond on the map for a little while, and that was when people were calling the place "Woolgar Cursed Park".

"How did the two boys have a head on collision" Gus asked Owen.

Adding a little more ice and pouring another scotch into the glass, Owen went into detail.

The police forensic people were all over the place, looking at tracks and the wrecks and taking both the quad bikes away for scrutiny. The only thing they found that may have been faulty and inoperable that night was on the quad bike that they believed was travelling to the south.

They finally came to the conclusion that the boys were heading home in the dark that night and that one of the boys who was travelling behind the other, and they didn't know which boy it was on which bike, they believe his headlight stopped working and that he stopped to try to fix it.
The boy in front would not have known that he had stopped and would have continued on his way home. It is believed that the boy could not get his light working and attempted to travel without it. The boy in front is presumed to have discovered that his brother was not following and turned around to go back to find him. They found the quad bike tracks to show this, it is believed that he may have been travelling very fast and on those turns would not have known or seen his brother, without a light on his bike and they both collided.

The forensic people also found that Curtis had died from decapitation, caused by not wearing a seat belt and having the window down, he was thrown towards the window and as the car rolled down the embankment, his head went through the window and was torn from his body.

How tragic, unbelievable, they all muttered finishing their drinks and after a brief conference, decided on more drinks, after all, it was only twelve thirty and no reason to get up early. All were also of the opinion that it could have indeed been a "curse".

"So, the whole family gone, then what happened to this property" asked Malcolm.
Well, me and Jenny had no idea what to do, Owen continued with his story on Woolgar River Park, as everyone settled down and got comfy, this time on the lounges and chairs that were pulled up together. They all agreed that Owen was a fantastic narrator and very easy to listen to.

The Police Sergeant who was in charge of the incident had suggested that we just get on with life until we hear from someone, most likely the family's solicitor.

Well, it seems the family did not have a will, or one that could be found and after about two months. We were thinking of leaving as we had not been paid since the accidents and we were running out of money and we had no idea of what to do and where to go.

Whilst deciding what to do, we had a visit from an officer from the Queensland Public Trustee. He arrived here with two other 'Assisting Officers' as he called them and they asked who we were and what did we have to do with the property and about a thousand other questions. He also wanted to know what our personal property was and did we had receipts, who owned the furniture in the house we were living in and stuff like that!.

He asked if we were prepared to stay and care for the property until it was sold, during which we would be paid remuneration back dated until the date of death of the owners at a rate that was about double what we had been getting, so our obvious answer was yes. The Officer also said that once they had surveyed the entire property they would send in people to conduct any repairs that were necessary to enable the sale of the property and also people to muster all the stock on the property for auction.

He said that all the items in the home would be assessed and any items that could be classified as valuable would be sold. Other items would be either sold or dumped after other surviving members of the family had seen if there were any items that could be claimed as theirs or any other items they wanted as family pieces. All furniture and fixtures, including washing machines, dryers, refrigerators, freezers, televisions, computers and office equipment would remain in the home to be included in the auction.

Lachlan Teague

So we had a fairly easy life around here for about two months until the property was sold, even then, after the sale, we were told it would be at least three months before the new owner would be here and we were again asked it we would stay on and paid the same by the new owner.

We couldn't see why not, life was being pretty good, the Public Trustee had been paying for two workers to look after the cattle, water bores and the fencing and we were on better pay than we ever had been. One of the workers they employed was our son, Barry, so things were really good for us, as sad as the situation that had got us into this position was.

Lachlan Teague, who had taken on his brother's former property, which was bought by his father, Campbell Teague, upon the departure of his brother Alisdair Teague, for Australia some years ago,

then his father's property upon his father's death, at the age of sixty one, had decided to sell these three properties and move to Australia and was actively looking for a cattle property there by means of the Internet. He had come across an advertisement for a property that was coming up for auction at a location near Hughenden in North Queensland, being the major centre and Richmond being a regional township, had taken his interest, to the extent of making some direct enquiries, via email to the auctioning agent at Townsville, also in Queensland. He had read as much as he could find out about the property, including estimated valuations, which to him seemed it may be a lucrative and stable investment.

He did ask the agent why it is, the property on the market, sounding like such a good investment and the reply was, that it is a deceased estate.

As the auction was to be held in Townsville, Lachlan then engaged a Solicitor who was also located in Townsville to act on his behalf and to purchase the property at the auction for up to three million dollars, and also to act as his Conveyancer up to settlement of the property and also to engage staff as necessary to maintain and operate the property until his arrival in Australia, the date to be advised. The auction day was at two pm on a Tuesday and Lachlan, at just after four am in the morning in Glasgow, received a call from his Townsville Solicitor, telling him he was the owner of" Woolgar River Park" at the cost of two point two million dollars Australian Dollars.

In the interim period of Lachlan leaving Scotland and arriving in Australia, he had made contact, via email with Owen Harrigan through his Townsville Solicitor, and confirmed that all was well in respect to staying on and that the remuneration was sufficient and to advise Lachlan if there were any problems with him or the property. He later advised Owen that he could expect some removal cartons within the next week or so and could he have them placed into his new home, anywhere would do for now and that he should be arriving within two weeks if all goes well.

Lachlan's flight departed Glasgow and made only one stop in Dubai before landing, thirty four hours later in Sydney Australia. He spent only one night in Sydney before getting a direct flight to Townsville. He booked in at the Casino for two nights, then called the BMW dealer for the area and suggested they might like to collect him from the Casino as he wished to buy a new car. They arrived within fifteen minutes and he had bought a demo model x5 that they had suggested was perfect for the roads he had told them he would be travelling. They had dropped him back at the Casino within one hour of picking him up and made arrangements to collect him at eight o clock the next morning to take him to collect his new BMWx5.

The next morning after collecting his new car and armed with a map and directions from the Sales Manager at the dealership, he headed off to "Woolgar River Park" where he drove up to the home stead at four thirty that afternoon and introduced himself to Owen Harrigan and his wife Jenny.

Owen thanked Lynette as she poured another drink for him as he continued his story about "Woolgar River Park". We were told by the Trustee the new owner was Lachlan Teague and that he would of course be in touch with us for our next directions.

Lachlan made contact by email a few times and told us the day he would be here, and he was.

He arrived at about four, four thirty in a flash looking set of wheels and we went out to meet him.

We didn't know what to expect and I think that when we saw the flash car pull up, then we thought the worst, you know, a new high and mighty sort of person, But we got a shock, this fellow was the nicest person that anyone could meet, he was so polite and very humble.

We addressed him as Mr Teague and he said Mr Teague was his father and he is dead, my name is Lachlan and that is what you should call me, he told them

Jenny had ordered by internet, a sheet set for a queen bed, some pillows and a light doona from a shop in Townsville when we had notice of Lachlan's arrival and as fate would have it they had arrived in time. She had also turned on a refrigerator in the kitchen and had put some long life milk into it, she had also bought some tea, coffee and sugar along with some cream biscuits.

We took Lachlan over to the big house. Jenny had made sure it was clean but other than furniture, there was nothing there. Jenny said that she had made up the bed in one room, just until he got sorted, and there is tea and coffee in the kitchen and milk in the fridge. Then she told him that they were expecting him for dinner that night.

Lachlan had thanked them both so much on that first night, he was beside himself for the few things we had done for him. Owen told everyone that Lachlan certainly enjoyed scotch whiskey and helped Owen to clean up the two bottles of Johnny Walker red label that he had, plus about a dozen beers. During our conversation, Jenny asked when his wife would be arriving, but we had already guessed that he didn't have one. Lachlan just said, no wife, no kids, no worries, in his broad Scott's accent. It was like we had known each other for ages, it was just great..

For the next two weeks, it was full on with Lachie, as we had begun to call him. We all drove down to Townsville and stayed at the Casino for three nights to help him do shopping for the items he required for his home, and stacked as much food into the Beamer as we could. The following week it was more shopping around Charters Towers and Hughenden. It was full on and we were enjoying it. Nearly every second day we were down at Alice's pub having lunch and drinks of course, so many times Jenny had to drive us home because Lachie and I had drunk too much.

"Speaking of" interjected Lynette, "we are out of Scotch, you'll have to have beer if you want another drink and I actually think that there is not too much of that left fellows and I am heading to bed" and then added, "Are you right to get home Owen, or do you want to stay here somewhere"

Owen said that the landrover knew its way home and thanked Lynette and Gus for a fantastic meal and thanked everyone for their fantastic company and that we should all do it again one day.

And with that, he staggered out of the front door waving as he went.

They could hear the Landrover until he just about got home so they knew he was alright.

Following a breakfast of sausages, Sunday morning meant a grog run into Richmond and the three men went in Malcolm's cruiser down to Richmond at about ten thirty that morning and the talk of course was about the whole family that had died on "Woolgar River Park" and how tragic.

Gus said to Malcolm that if he had known this prior to moving in then he may have chosen to sell the property and that he still might. Graham asked Gus if he was worried about the "curse" and did he believe in that sort of shit. Gus replied that the "curse" seemed to have taken out a whole family, how else would you explain that Graham?

"And could the "curse" be responsible for the death of the 'Parks' following owner Lachlan"? added Gus, "I had forgotten to show you the twenty two case we found in the bedroom, we'll do that when we get back" he added, "I thought that Lynette was getting paranoid about the used casing but after hearing all this, well, we'll see what you guys think"!

After they had bought more cartons of beer, sauvignon blanc, riesling and two more bottles of scotch, they went into the bar for dust clearing beer, which went down fairly slow but got better on the second beer. The bar was quiet and Alice asked Gus how he was settling in and commented that they all looked a bit crook this morning.

Gus mentioned that they had met up with Owen Harrigan and he had told them all about the tragic end of the Southwells out at "Woolgar River Park. "Oh god, that was so awful, that it was actually unbelievable how a family of five could die within a few weeks of each other, some people around here believe it was the "curse" that the Aboriginal had put on the family" Alice responded.
"The town was buzzing, we had Sixty Minutes out here, Four Corners, it was great for the pub while it lasted but it fizzed out and you don't hear anything about it these days, that must have been about nearly eighteen years ago" Alice continued, "nothing else has happened in all that time at the 'park' other than poor old Lachie passing, but that was just old age, nothing to do with curses."

They finished their beers and went back to the 'Park' as Alice called it.

Malcolm reversed down to the back door of the laundry for easy access to the cool room and they unloaded his car. The ladies were relaxing on the verandah and discussing the last night's revelations no doubt Gus supposed, and he suggested that Lynette demonstrate to every one the used twenty two cartridge case.

They all went up to the master bedroom and Lynette began to recount the events leading up to the discovery of the used casing. Then she put forward her theory of what she thought could have been possible which brought gasps from everyone. It seemed very logical to all, especially Graham Jamison who seemed to be in a trance as he moved from side to side of the bed, just staring at the drapes and finally omitted a big "Yes, I most definitely concur Lynette" Graham said while still staring at the drapes and asked if there were any gaps between the flooring and the skirting board anywhere in the room.

Everyone just seemed to automatically look around the room at the floor and wall junction. Graham was down looking under the bed and called out for a torch. Lynette found the torch they kept in the walk in robe and passed it to Graham, who was still under the bed. He finally extracted himself, stood up and announced that there was a gap in the floor under the skirting of about 7~8mm high and about 50mm long. He then asked if that meant anything to anyone, grinning while waiting for someone to respond. Lynette was about to answer his question correctly but thought she would not "steal his thunder".

"The gap, ladies and gentlemen", said Graham playfully grandstanding, "would indicate that Lynette's theory is correct. If someone had fired an automatic .22 pistol into this bed and then tried to locate the ejected, spent case and could not find it, but discovered this gap, they may well believe the cartridge case to have rolled into it as the case is only a bit over 5mm thick and would look no further, otherwise if no gap was found then the person, I would assume, would keep searching the entire room and would most likely look towards the drapes during their search".

Very plausible suggested Gus, and all agreed. "Does that mean" asked Ros, "that someone murdered Lachlan" "It means" said Graham, "that some person has definitely fired a shot, or maybe more, into this bed, and why would anyone do that to a bed? I would believe because a person lay there as there are, as you say, Lynette, no bullet holes in the mattress. All jokes aside, this could be very serious Graham had concluded".

The discussion that afternoon was mainly the spent casing, although Graham was of the opinion that it may indeed be a case for investigation. The only way to prove the theory would be to exhume Lachlan's body for the purpose of an autopsy, but finding a spent twenty two cartridge case in a bedroom seemed like a feeble reason for exhuming a body. Catch twenty two? Hmm.

During the dinner conversation that evening, Graham also suggested that there were, or seemed to be some weird happenings following Lachlan's death that certainly warranted some looking into and who knows, maybe also prior to Lachlan's death. "I will certainly be looking a little more into Sonia Teague", said Graham. Gus Interrupted Graham at that point to say that her name, from what they have heard, may not indeed be Sonia Teague, but Sonia Harris. Sadly, Monday morning had arrived and that meant packing up and heading home for Malcolm and Ros, and also for Graham and Stefanie.

Graham was taking the spent .22 casing with him to run some tests, firstly for fingerprints and secondly to find the manufacturer of the pistol that fired it through the firing pin indent, hopefully.

All had agreed that they did not want to leave and had suggested the same again on the next weekend, or even take holidays out here and enjoy the countryside and the great company.

They were truly now all friends and Jamison's were already making plans to meet up with the Davies when back in Townsville.

Gus and Lynette waved goodbye to their friends and wandered back to their favourite spot on the verandah.

"What are you thinking" Gus asked Lynette, noticing that look of doubt in her eyes, "Oh Gus, I really don't know what to think". "I do know that I would not have moved into here if I was aware of all the tragedy that has occurred here. This morning when I left our bedroom, I looked down the hallway and I could imagine the children, well, grown children walking from their rooms to go downstairs for breakfast, it was horrible".

Lynette had continued with her feelings, saying how beautiful she thought the house and the property was when she had first seen it. The news that someone was trying to sell it didn't deter her, even the spent cartridge case and the possibility of a murder taking place in their own bedroom, although it did somewhat phase her, she could cope with that.
It was the knowledge that a whole family had died here within a matter of days between them, three of them on one night, that gave her a very uneasy feeling. The "curse" the Aboriginal had placed on the family, was it on the property also, really? Was the "curse" really responsible for the deaths of all the family members, really?

If you had read about the events leading to the tragedy it all seems possible, flukey, but possible, even uncanny, but possible, but add a black fella's "curse" to it all and it just seems ridiculous. "I just don't know if I want to live here anymore Gus, I do want to find out more about the place though and especially about the mystery of the spent casing,

I think there may have been a murder, but I suppose bottom line is, I want to get to the bottom line of all of these little bugs and mysteries that we seem to have" Lynette admitted.

Gus agreed with her. He too had developed a bit of a weird feeling about the house now that he was aware of what had transpired there. But, you also need to remember, that all happened seventeen years ago and other than the passing of Lachlan, he didn't think there had been any other tragedies, other than this bitch Sonia, whom they both had intentions of finding out what exactly was happening, or happened and they were sure to sort that out.

In the interim, they both agreed to hang in and sort it all out, having said that, Gus called on Willem and asked him to bring the step ladder to the laundry stairs landing where the access panel to the ceiling area is located. "We'll sort out this wifi," Gus told Willem.
Gus went and found his LED torch while Willem was fetching the steps and they met at the access panel. Gus was not keen on ceiling spaces even though it was a major part of his job as a Building Surveyor, he just did not like them.

Gus went up the steps and flipped up the access panel then placed it carefully inside the ceiling on a batten. Standing on the very top of the steps, he reached up and held on to a truss strut and slowly pulled himself up and into the ceiling area and shone his light around the ceiling space.

Very neat, he thought as he saw the fifty millimetre planks spanning the roof truss chords at nine hundred millimetres centres for the full length of the centre of the roof, following the hallway below.

He knew roughly where the satellite aerial was located on the roof and he aimed the torch in that direction and could instantly see the cables coming down from the aerial. He had to walk the full length of the walkway, and then across to his right, then leaving the plank walkway and keeping his feet to the truss chords, he worked his way across to the cables. There were two cables, one was a power cord and the other was an ethernet cable which he followed with his light.

The cable was laid loosely on the truss chords and went behind the brick chimney. Gus slowly worked his way following the cable along to where it turned around the brickwork. There sat the modem next to a powerpoint fixed to a strut. Taking his mobile phone out of his pocket, then squatting down to the modem, Gus turned the modem over to reveal its password, using his mobile telephone he then took a clear photo of the password.

As Gus was slowly starting to stand up and looking with his light for his best passage back to the walkway, he glanced around at the general condition of the roof trusses, roof chords which were all hardwood and ceiling battens were pressed metal as was the partition stud framing. Good choice for this area Gus thought, as the termites around here he supposed were horrific from what he had seen with gates and fencing. The roof from this side looked good too and all seemed in a very sound condition he was thinking.

As he regained the walkway and was heading back to the access cover, he was looking at the outline of the partitions on his left and could make out the void areas where the dropped ceiling of the wardrobes in the queen rooms was at the far end of the building. He was almost at the access panel when he noticed that there was no dropped ceiling void in the last queen room.

He shone his light across towards where the void should have been.

From up in the ceiling area it appeared there was no wardrobe in that room, but he knew there was. Strange how things happen though, as that showed a high ceiling would be in that wardrobe. It may have been an error during the home construction and in particular the partitioning and linings.

Getting down from a ceiling was always good. Willem was waiting patiently and Lynette had joined him. "Well, what treasures did you discover up there", Lynette asked, Gus negatively shook his head whilst drawing a breath, "It's as clean as up there, just one peculiar thing which I am about to check now though" as he headed across the hallway towards the first queen room.

Both Willem and Lynette followed as Gus went into the room and went straight up to the wardrobe. The wardrobes in the first queen room was to the left hand side and you walked into the room, there were two wardrobes on each side to the ensuite entry, and the robes faced into the bedroom with mirrored doors on each side of the 900 millimetre wide walkthrough, each wardrobe was fifteen hundred millimetres wide with a transom above the walkway at twenty one hundred millimetres high and six hundred millimetres wide, to match the depth of the wardrobe on each side.

The architectural effect as you looked at the robes from inside the room, was a large mirrored door on each side and a painted sliding door in the centre, that when opened revealed the ensuite. Very smart idea and makes the room look so much tidier as there is no indication of an ensuite.

Gus looked up at the walkthrough ceiling, it had a white timber frame all around the walkthrough ceiling.

Gus went into the next queen room. In this one, the robes were to the right of the room and they appeared to be identical, but when he looked up at the walkthrough ceiling, this ceiling was flush set plasterboard. But, it did not have a timber frame. Gus checked the wardrobe in the last queen room and the walkthrough ceiling was also flush set plasterboard.

Lynette asked Gus what the hell was he doing, but Gus only gave her the "you'll see" look.

Gus went back to the first room and moved the chair from the desk over to the walkthrough. Standing on the chair, Gus pushed up on the ceiling between the white timber framing and the ceiling moved away from the white timber framing, similar to an access panel.

Gus placed the panel over to the right side wardrobe and shone his light into the ceiling area above the right side wardrobe. Plywood had been placed on the dropped ceiling framing to form a shelf.

"Anything in there Gus", asked Lynette and Gus responded, "It may be the missing rifles" and he reached in to grab one.

"NO, NO Gus, don't touch anything, there could be good prints on those, I'll get you some rubber gloves" Lynette said, already on her way to the kitchen, but came back and said that it might be an idea to leave them there until she talks to Graham.

Gus abandoned the idea of getting hold of a rifle and shone his light on the other side. There he could see a timber box and he called down to Lynette and told her about the box, its dimensions, were approximately three hundred and fifty millimetres long and two hundred wide and one hundred deep with a name on top. She asked what was the name but Gus could not read it as it was facing upside down to him. Lynette told him to use his handkerchief to turn it around toward him. As he turned the box around, he could see a leather carry strap and two black clasps and he read out the name on the front M A R G O L I N M C M. Not having a notepad with her she typed it into her memo on her mobile telephone. Gus continued to say there was a shot shell belt and some Winchester X shot shell boxes and some other, smaller boxes behind them, but he could not see them properly. He then got down from the chair and said "Interesting", to Lynette.

"So, I wonder who Margolin, MCM is? More mysteries," said Gus.
Willem looked at Gus and asked, "Did you get dar wi fi passwords no", Gus just looked at him and laughed, "I'll text it to you".

Lynette said she would contact Graham tomorrow and tell him what they had discovered today and ask his advice. She would ask him if he could come up and take prints from the rifles and the mysterious box.

Tuesday came and Gus contacted Peter Lansky at the stock agents in Richmond and apologised for not getting back to him last week. But you know how things turn out, I just ran out of time he added and then asked if Peter could assess the property this week and they could get things happening. Peter's response was good as he was in contact with a company looking to agist out about three thousand head as soon as possible. He could most likely get out there tomorrow afternoon. Gus said he would look forward to seeing him.

Gus then took a drive down the track to see Owen, whom he found doing something under the bonnet of the old Landrover. Owen, hearing the Landcruiser drive up, got from under the bonnet and said to Gus, "If you've come for a cold beer, then you're in luck".

"Sounds like a plan to me" replied Gus, following Owen to his verandah. Owen went inside and came back with two xxxx gold stubbies.

They sat on the verandah and Owen mentioned the great night and thanked him for the great food and drink. Owen promised to return the favour and get him and Lynette around for dinner before too long.

Gus told Owen about the cattle agistment idea and Owen told Gus that he thought agistment was a good way to go. But he would need some good people to look after the cattle, pumps and fences. Gus told him that was why he was here, to offer Owen the job.

Owen said he was too old for doing that sort of work now, but that he could organise a crew for him, in return for rent here at this house. He said that he had his son, Barry in mind and two of his mates. He knew that Gus had people living in the Manager's House and that was fine as Barry would stay with him here, and that the other fellas would camp at the other house up at the
Homestead.

Owen said though, that Gus would be better off getting the agistment herd up to max. at about six to seven thousand, as it would only take one extra hand to look after that amount. More dollars for the bank account that way, he grinned.

Gus told him about Peter Lansky coming out tomorrow arvo and Owen said "That thieving prick Lansky, you'd be better off with Dillons at Hughenden. They are fairly straight to deal with, but just steer this prick around to me tomorrow before you let him look around, I'll sort him out".

Gus said, "Owen, you're on, but I insist on a wage as well as the house, I don't want anyone working here for nothing".

"At my age, I won't be doing too much Gus, that'll be the fella's job, but I'll see it all gets done properly and if you insist that I get a wage, well I don't want to get on the wrong side of you now and cause ill feelings, so you pay me whatever you feel is fair" said Owen, holding out his right hand to shake Gus's. Two more beers and then Gus headed back home feeling a lot happier and thought, "fuck the curse". This could be a good business and it seemed that Owen was the man to have looking after the agistment business, and maybe Willem can be useful with them also as the extra man that Owen spoke of.

Graham Jamison was listening to Lynette talk about the rifles that had been found in a secret little storage area. Lynette suggested that Graham might want to fingerprint them. Graham's interest was really waning, as the test result on the cartridge had not yet been revealed, if it had in fact been carried out yet. He couldn't really get the lab guys too excited as they had a heap of work on and Graham's job was not official.

Graham was still sort of half listening as Lynette mentioned the box, but he sat bolt upright when she mentioned the name on the box. He said to her, "Spell that again", and then he said "Margolin was the make of a Russian target pistol", he asked if there was a pistol in the box. Lynette did not know as they had not opened the box, it still lay in the hidden ceiling space.
Lynette told Graham that they didn't touch anything for fear of spoiling any prints that may be on the items, everything is just how they found it.

Graham suggested that Lynette, wearing gloves should get the box down and see if the pistol is in fact in the box. If it is, then he will get a police courier to collect the pistol and take it to Townsville for ballistic tests to see if the spent case came from that pistol. Also, he will send with the police courier a print kit so Lynette can dust for prints on the rifles, then take photos of all prints and forward them by email to Graham. He also asked when was a good time for the courier to collect to which Lynette said "Anytime, get them to call me first". Graham said to call him back as soon as she knew if the pistol was in the box.

Donning disposable kitchen gloves, Lynette took her set of household steps up to the first queen room and removed the box. She knew by the weight that it did most likely contain the pistol.

Downstairs in the office she placed the box on the desk and undid the clasps on each side of the leather carry handle and opened the lid to reveal a most elegant looking black target pistol, very similar to a Luger pistol at first glance. The pistol itself was in its dedicated compartment within the box, another section held two magazines, one of them loaded with cartridges, and separate sections held various items such as cleaning rod, barrel weights, oil bottle, and small screwdriver. She carefully closed the box and called Graham back.

The following day, Peter Lansky had called Gus to say he was on the way over, just about the time a constable Kathy Green had called Lynette to see if she could collect an item for Townsville Ballistics.

The constable was the first to arrive in her brightly coloured highway patrol car at about midday after driving the five hundred kilometres from Townsville that morning. She handed Lynette the fingerprint kit and she had a chat with Lynette, obviously, previously being told that Lynette was an ex police sergeant. She also enjoyed a coffee and a toasted sandwich before heading straight back to Townsville with the box containing the Margolin.

The Agistment Stock

Peter Lansky arrived just as the marked police car was departing and gave Gus a quizzical look as he went to meet him, "just one of Lynette's police friends dropping by" Gus remarked, "hop in the cruiser and I'll take you around to see Owen".

"Owen" Peter said questionably, "I thought Barry would have been the man to show me the grazing conditions". Gus assured Peter that Barry would in fact be in charge of all the grazing, watering and welfare of the agistment, but Owen will be overseeing the entire operation, including the agistment conditions and costings. Peter Lansky did not look too happy with this arrangement.

They arrived at Owen's and sat at the table on the verandah to commence the negotiations. Gus would have preferred his newly acquired, impressive looking office at the homestead for this type of thing but Owen didn't think that Lansky rated high enough for the office, banker's psychology Owen had said.

Owen nodded his head towards Peter and said good afternoon then made it quite clear that we are looking at a minimal six thousand head of cattle. If we can't talk around the four dollars and fifty cents per head mark, plus any veterinaries and less any stock transports by road and all as per Animals Care and Protection Act 2001, then it would be a waste of a trip for Peter today, "and that sir, is straight to the point" added Owen.

Lansky told Owen that he didn't have six thousand head at the moment but rather just over four thousand head. Owen responded that we would need around the five dollars fifty mark for less than six thousand. Peter Lansky, looking a little perplexed agreed to five fifty for four thousand but said that he would get it up to six thousand within a month or so and would then expect the rate to decrease to four fifty. "It will need to be six thousand" Owen said, "not five thousand nine hundred and ninety nine mind you".

Peter Lansky agreed, he pulled out the contract form and they started to complete it. When it came to the period of agistment, it was for six months with options, then the commencement date. Owen said that agistment availability would be in two weeks time.

Peter Lansky was hoping to start next week with the first road trains containing one hundred and ten bullocks each and looking at five road trains per day, which is all he could get at this stage so it would take him nearly two full weeks to get the four thousand on site.

Owen agreed telling Lansky to go for it, we'll be ready. We'll just have to get a bit more road base down in front of the yards following the last wet.. It was all done.

Owen had contacted his son Barry and told him to come out to meet Gus next Saturday as both Gus and Lynette would be at Owen's place for a BBQ. Lynette and Gus had no knowledge of that but when told they agreed it would be good and looked forward to it.

It was Friday morning when Lynette had received the call from Graham Jamison telling her that the spent cartridge she had found in the bedroom had in fact been fired in the Margolin that they had found in the house and that the police were currently seeking a court order to have the body of Lachlan Teague exhumed.

Graham asked her not to make it public knowledge and asked how she had got on with prints. Lynette had told Graham that she would get them done today. Graham said that the forensics would be in Richmond for the exhumation at the Richmond cemetery and he would get them to do them if she liked, to which she agreed as she had never really done much with prints other than during her training countless years ago. Gus just shook his head when Lynette had told him.

Dinner on Saturday night was a BBQ at Owens and was a great evening. They had finally got to meet Barry who, although seemed to be very slow, was such a lovely and friendly person. He was a big man though seemed to be over gentle but was extremely grateful to get his old job back.
After dinner, there was of course drinks on the verandah on that lovely warm evening. Barry was a non drinker and must have drunk a half carton of Coke cans during the evening until he went to bed where he was staying with Owen.

Lynette happened to ask Owen about Sonia Teague. Owen responded that she was not really Teague, she seemed to have adopted the name off her own bat. She was never ever married to Lachie nor was she living with him. In fact, Lachie had often told Owen that he wished he'd never employed her, and that if she was not so efficient doing her job as a housekeeper she would have gone ages ago. She didn't live in the main house but lived in the other two bedroom house. Lachie would not have her living in there although she kept coming up with excuses to move into there.

It was only in the last year or so really that, when Lachlan started to become ill, that she seemed to take over everything. I think that was when she started to call herself Sonia Teague whilst ordering goods to be delivered to the property and tradespeople to visit.
Owen said that he had heard in the pub in Richmond that she had been telling people that she and Lachlan were secretly married a couple of years back.

But during the last year, she had turned into a real Bitch. The big house was always open and I would quite often stroll in and have breakfast with Lachie, and we would get on the piss some afternoons or evenings, but all of a sudden, or so as it seemed, the house was locked. I would knock on the door and Sonia would answer with her finger to her lips saying shhhh, Lachlan is not very well this morning and that went on and on the extent that I only went over to the house when I had to. But I tell you, she had taken over. I think I only saw Lachie about twice before he died and by god he did look crook, and as he started to talk he would start coughing and could not finish saying whatever it was he was trying to say.

Lachie said it was ulcers. He said that his Doctor wanted to remove them, but Lachie had told the Doctor that he would not have an operation and so instead he had placed Lachie on a medicine, that would in time clear the ulcers away. Owen said that he had never heard of such a medicine.
He seemed to be that way for at least a year and then one morning Sonia came down to the Manager's House and announced that Lachlan had died.
I will never forget how she just said it in such a matter of fact sort of tone. "Fucking Bitch".

Barry came up to the house to see Gus the morning before the first of the cattle were due to arrive and told him that the worker who was supposed to have started work that morning had not shown and that it was unlikely that he would show. He went on to say that his father had said that Gus had a worker here that he could use. Gus said that he did and took Barry down to meet Willem, who had very little to do since arriving here. The girls, Hailee and Janice were busy every day, it seemed helping Lynette with cleaning and painting and all sorts of jobs around the house, but Willem did not really have a job other than going into Richmond from time to time on errands for the girls.

Barry told Willem that he needed help doing bore runs and maintenance on the fences. Willem was only too happy to have something to do. Barry then said to Gus that he would need a station vehicle and that Willem would also need a station vehicle and that when the cattle get here we will need some quaddies. He said he thought Dad would have mentioned that.

Gus was going to suggest that Barry would get his ute back but thought twice about it as he had become quite attached to it. He told Barry that he would get on to some additional vehicles for the property this afternoon, and asked Barry what type of quaddies would they need.

Barry said Yamaha 250 Grizzly's 4wd as it gets greasy here when wet.

Gus called around looking for used Landcruiser Utes and only found two at Charters Towers Toyota, one was a fairly new 2018 but it was top of the line with a steel body as opposed to alloy and had the two bucket seats, rather than the standard three seats and electric windows, air conditioning and cruise control and the other a 2000. Gus told the guy he would take them both and a deal was struck. Gus did a bank transfer to the motor dealer and said he would collect them on Wednesday.

He then got onto a quad bike motorcycle's dealer, also in Charters Towers and they had several of the quad bikes in stock and did an attractive deal for three bikes. Gus paid for them by direct transfer and said he would collect them on Wednesday.

Gus told Barry that he could have his old ute back and he was thrilled to get it back. Gus told him that the three of them, meaning Willem, Barry & Gus, would be going to Charters Towers tomorrow to collect two more Utes and three quaddies. Barry was impressed and said it was great to see things happening around here again.

Gus was having a beer on the verandah that afternoon and working on his laptop. He was setting up a spreadsheet for the incoming agistment herd which looked like eighty eight thousand dollars for the first month then five hundred and ninety five thousand dollars for the five months after. That's six hundred and seventy five thousand dollars for six months, pretty good.

Gus went into the office and turned on the Mac desktop and started to look through it. He found that it had a spreadsheet program similar to excel installed on it, and opened it up to find lots of excel type files called 'stock2009' and running up to 'stock2016' but they were protected and he could not open these files. He also saw worksheet files labelled balance sheet 'such and such' year, these were also protected.

He browsed around looking at various items and then went into a word type program, here there were lots of files containing correspondence. Gus noticed a word sub directory called SH which was also protected.

Whilst wondering what may be within the locked files, Gus also wondered about the mobile telephone they had found. I must get it opened he was thinking, then thought that Hailee was the IT expert he would ask her and also about the locked files.

Wednesday morning found Gus driving with Barry and Willem all cramped into the front of the Landcruiser heading to Charters Towers, a good four hours drive. They had left at six am that morning and were hoping to get back home at around three o'clock that afternoon.
Arriving at the Toyota dealer, Gus and Willem stayed there to pick up the two Utes and would meet Barry at the Yamaha dealers just down the road.
Gus met the salesman whom he had made a deal with and sorted out the vehicle's registration details while Willem took the year 2000 cruiser to find Barry and load a quad bike on the back.

The salesman remembered the name Teague as Lachlan had bought the other, 2006 model from him as a new vehicle and was sad, he said, to hear of his passing.
Gus had to buy six pairs of ratchet tie downs from the quad bike dealer to tie down the quad bikes on each ute. The dealer asked if we had ramps at the property to get them off and Barry told him that we have a loading ramp. Gus thought at least that was something else that we did not have to buy, not quite understanding why the Dealer could not have

thrown in the tie down straps. He had bought three new bikes from him and he knew that replacement quad bikes would not be bought from here! Twenty four thousand dollars for three bikes and he could not even throw in thirty six bucks worth of tie down straps. At least the Toyota guy filled both the Utes up with about two hundred dollars worth of diesel. "Fuck you pal".

Gus was very impressed with his near new cruiser ute. This one only had two seats compared to the 2006 model's two and three quarter seat setup, and was much more comfortable, even the ride seemed smoother and this one also had air conditioning.

They arrived back about three thirty and both Gus and Willem followed Barry to the loading ramp which was behind the cattle yards. They unloaded the bikes then both the boys ferried two of the bikes back to the shed at the homestead then Gus took them back to the yard and left them to getting the last bike back, then their Utes.

Gus went back to the house after a long day of driving and relaxed with Lynette in the bar with a beer and Lynette asked where all the money was coming from to buy all these new Utes and quad bikes. Gus grabbed his laptop and showed her the spreadsheet he had started with the agistment stock coming in and was blown away with his predicted annual agistment turnover of one point four million dollars, he was still setting up the spreadsheet so at this stage gave no indicative costs but Gus said that even if you allow sixty per cent, which it should not be quite that much, then we are still looking at around six hundred thousand dollar profit, and those items will be tax offsets. Gus also said that he intended on asking Malcolm to recommend an accountant to look after the accounts as it is not within Gus's expertise.

The cattle had been arriving, everything seemed to be happening and everybody seemed happy, things were looking good, and both Lynette and Gus were starting to relax more.

A Case For Murder

Graham Jamison had called Lynette with somewhat chilling news, that a projectile had been found in the skull of Lachlan Teague. It's a .22 calibre projectile and the ballistic guys have matched the projectile with the Margolin target pistol that you found.
The ammunition is for target shooting at twenty five metres, it's a very low velocity round. It appears that the pistol was placed in his ear and then fired. The round would most likely have killed him instantly though the projectile did not exit, hence that is why we found it and that is why there is no hole in the mattress, nor bloodstains.

Fortunately, for me anyway, they have given me this job, so I will be up there in the morning with the forensic team to take some prints and photographs. Lynette asked if he wanted to stay here but Graham said that it would not be a good idea, not that Gus and Lynette were suspects which they are not, but just to keep things above board. Graham did say however that if he did happen to stay for dinner and have too many drinks, well...shit happens.

Lynette was shocked but strangely not really as she had suspected a shooting when she had discovered the casing, and was further convinced of a shooting when they found the pistol.
Graham had just confirmed her theory.

That's not all there is to it Lynette, as Graham continued. Whilst the body was exhumed various tests, that could still be conducted at that stage of decomposition, were applied and a strange substance that should not have been present was found called 'brodifacoum'.

"Have you heard of brodifacoum Lynette?" asked Graham.

"It rings a bell, It's a fairly common substance isn't it"

"It's very common" Lynette, "It's found in rat poison, probably there is some in everybody's house, but people don't generally eat it to such an extent that was discovered in the remains of Lachlan's body".

Lynette was stunned, bad enough with a bullet let alone poison, well, we'll have plenty to chat about tomorrow when I see you, Graham.

Lynette just had to break the news to Gus whom she thought was out at the cattle yards. She hopped into the Subaru that was parked next to the BMW, which made her remember the new key with the transponder had arrived last week but everyone had been too busy to try it out.

She locked the Subaru back up and went back to the house to get the new key.

It started instantly, she didn't know how long it had been sitting here for but the fuel tank showed almost full, the pale tan looking leather seats felt so soft and comfortable. She put it into reverse and it purred like a kitten as it reversed out of the driveway. Very cool she thought, when she noticed the camera with all round vision which turned off as she selected drive, hmmm she thought nice car. I might just call this mine she thought, after all, she had the one and only key.

She headed out cautiously and once over the homestead entrance grid she turned to the left to head towards the cattle yards about six kilometres away. She gave, what the dual turbos were waiting for, the accelerator a slight nudge, and the car literarily took off, woo woo she giggled as she eased back on the accelerator, "this little baby wants to boogey" she said out loud to nobody. She added a touch more throttle just to get a bit used to it, my, what a machine, she thought, my machine now!

She arrived at the cattle yards to find two road trains waiting to unload, there were already at least two hundred, she guessed, cattle in the yards and a road train just departing. She saw Gus's new landcruiser parked next to Barry's and headed that way. She hadn't been able to get Gus out of his new ute, as he called it, he just loved it.

Gus walked over as she pulled up, "I wondered who the fucking hell it was when I saw the car" he said, "nice looking wheels you have there miss"
"Well don't look too hard brother because these wheels are mine, you've got your ute and I have my beamer" Then seriously she said, "You'd better come home, I have some big news".

They sat on the verandah with icy beers as Lynette started to tell Gus the news about the murder investigation that was now underway, she left nothing out of Graham's phone call and concluded with he will here tomorrow morning. "Well fuck me, you were fucking on to that from the moment you found that casing" he leaned across and kissed her, "You're a fucking legend Lynette and I am so proud of you, I mean like, fuck me, if anyone else had found that casing, it would have been in the bin and if you weren't here I would have been out shooting with that fucking gun. Good on you"

Gus said, he was also sad that his uncle's life had been shortened by that Bitch, but Lynette cut him short saying that no one knows who killed his uncle so he can't go around saying things like that. Gus had said, well who else, and Lynette quipped that you have to wait and see what transpires. "London to a brick, it's that Bitch, I'll bet"."Would you bet your new ute on it" laughed Lynette."No, not my new ute, but I still bet it's her". "Well, we'll hopefully find out, it's your shout"

Graham had arrived, alone in his unmarked police car just after ten am the next morning and his forensic team about half an hour later. Quick hello's were had and they all got down to business starting with the concealed area above the queen room's ensuite entry. They were all stunned at how Gus could have possibly found it, some of the Forensic Officers viewed Gus suspiciously at his skill to expose the ceiling.

Even when Gus took them up into the ceiling area and showed them what, to him, revealed something strange down below, the Forensic people were at a complete loss as they said, that it did not look suspicious to them. Gus thought that they were as dumb as dog shit for not identifying such an error in construction. He showed them how the robe ceilings were a dropped ceiling by pointing to the other two queen room wardrobe areas in the ceiling. They all looked, and then he showed them how this particular robe ceiling was not dropped.

"Well how do you know there is a void under it if you can't see it" asked a Senior Sergeant.

Gus thought that they really thought that he knew all about the hidden areas.

"You must have known there was a place to hide things, how would anyone know by just looking, it's impossible" the same Sergeant went on, Gus just gave up.

They took about three thousand photographs of the ceiling area and the concealed area above the walkthrough. They photographed the rifles about twenty times before they even moved them to place them into their special police hi ace van. They dusted for fingerprints all over the access panel and the removable ceiling section.

Then, they all had to see the bedroom where the cartridge case was discovered and Lynette had to repeat the whole series of events at least nine times. They took pictures of the drapes and the bed and the widow frame, Lynette had to pull back the bed sheets to expose the mattress.

And just when Gus and Lynette had thought they were finished, they took photos of the kitchen and dusted for prints in the kitchen and around the butler's pantry, the dining area, the front entry and all around the house perimeter. Finally, after about five hours they departed in their van to Hughenden where they were staying, and said they had at this stage concluded taking in any more evidence and would not likely to be returning.

Once they had left, Graham had suggested a meeting on the verandah. Lynette, knowing that Graham was officially working offered him a coke, "Please tell me you are joking Lynette, after driving up here for five hours and putting up with those boffins for five hours, I really think something rather more substantial may be more benefiting"
Lynette handed Graham a cold beer and asked Gus if he was ready for another, whilst passing one to him.

Graham said that he that he would like to interview Owen tomorrow in respect to Sonia, whatever her name might be. Lynette brought over more beers as Graham dug a file out of his laptop bag and passing it over to Lynette said, "Have a read of this, it's Jason Strange's statement and declaration". Lynette read it out for all to hear.

Qld Police: Statement from Jason Strange:

Mrs Teague first made contact with me on a Tuesday of March 2021 in respect to placing her property on the market. She gave a brief description of the property and said she could email me a much more precise description and photographs of the four dwellings on the property and wanted a quick sale and would settle for exactly two point one million dollars, then asked if I would broker the sale.

I told her it was not quite that simple and that firstly we must find out some facts before we would talk about figures and I suggested she send to me what she had in the form of a description and as many photos that she had, then I would make a time to meet her at the property and I would bring with me a sales engagement contract for her to sign.
I asked is the property solely in one name, and she said it was in two names, hers and her husband's Lachlan Teague.
She sent through the email and photos and I was most impressed and actually I could not wait to get it listed. The only way an Estate Agent makes money is on a quick sale with no messing around.

Looking at the photos and her description I knew this place would sell quickly and I have a mate who is a Solicitor that mainly only does Conveyancing. I contacted him and told him about this great opportunity where we could make a couple of million dollars each. We form a Company with the both of us as Directors, buy this property the moment it is listed, keep it for two years to avoid Capital Gains Tax, and then sell it for around seven to eight million. This was a golden opportunity, I could rake up a million and one hundred and he could do the same. We decided to do it.

His name is Richard Kemp, his office is in Firebrace Street, Horsham Victoria.

I contacted Mrs Teague and made an appointment to see her and went out to the property.

She had one of her workers, Barry drive me around the property and then she showed me, from the outside only as they were tenanted by the workers, the Manager's Cottage and the two bedroom cottage and saying how the other two bedroom cottage a distance away from the homestead, was identical and that I should have seen on my tour with Barry.

She then showed me through the main house. The downstairs areas first and then the upstairs, there was one room that I could not see as her sister was staying this month and sadly was feeling ill today, but she told me it was almost identical to the other king room.

She told me the property would be sold bare of stock and machinery and the furniture would be negotiable with the buyer.

We sat down at the table on the verandah and she got me a coke while I pretended to do some figures on my laptop and asked her to confirm bits and pieces. She was looking pretty anxious so I said that if may be a push to two point one, but one point eight, maybe nine should do it.

I wanted this, it was better that I had imagined and I could see a huge profit from this one, so I told her. Let's go for two point three and see what we get.

Mrs Teague was delighted and agreed, she said she would get Mr Teague from the cattle yards to come and sign the contract, while I prepare the sales appointment and marketing and sales contracts forms. I saw her walk over to the Manager's House and talk to Barry who got into his ute and drove away to return a few minutes later with Mr Teague. He certainly looked a bit scruffy from what I had imagined and compared to the way Mrs Teague was dressed. She said to me as he walked up to us, don't talk too much and don't ask any questions as he is suffering from Alzheimer's and it will only confuse him. Just point to where he has to sign, ok? She said that with such a lovely smile.

Mr Teague walked up and looked at me and said where do I sign, I showed him the five areas and he just signed them as I flipped the pages and pointed. When he had finished, he said is that all and he turned around and walked back to Barry's ute, got in and was driven away. Mrs Teague then sighed next to Mr Teague's signature and I witnessed them all.

Yes, it did seem strange to me, but I could not care less. I had the listing that was going to make me very rich. I called Mrs Teague after a week and said I have a contract on your property and I don't think she understood what I was saying as she said yes, you were here last week.

I said, Mrs Teague, I have sold your property, I have a contract for sale if you will accept two point one million dollars. She said to me yes that's what she wanted for it and I said I will drive out tomorrow with the contract for them to accept and sign. I told her I would be there around late morning and she said that no one has been out to look at the property yet and I said I will explain when I see her.

I tell you, I was pretty keen to get that contract of sale signed and I had it signed the next day.

She sat me at the verandah, gave me another coke but, this time she called Mr Teague on his mobile and soon after he turned up on the verandah where he signed as I indicated and then, like last time, he was gone. She signed and I witnessed, all done. SOLD!!

When I had asked her for her solicitor's name she told me she would have to call me back with that info. Seeing an opportunity, I said I know of one who specialises in Conveyancing. I could refer you to him if you wish. I also added that he is a straightforward type of Solicitor who has no time for all the pomp and colour and will accept most things by email, if you are interested.

Mrs Teague said that the Solicitor that I had mentioned would be fine, after all, it's only Conveyancing, isn't it?

Well, as is known, we were about a week away from settlement and it all fell to shit and I was exposed for inside trading and I am awaiting to be charged for that and many other associated criminal offences.

My friend in Horsham has also been arrested and is facing similar charges.

I Jason Strange of Charters Towers in the state of Queensland do solemnly swear that the above statement is a true and solemn statement from me signed at the law courts of Australia at Townsville 2021

"Wow, you have been busy Graham" said Lynette, being quite impressed so far.

"Well, that's the reason I need to talk to Owen, we think he may have been posing as Mr Teague and signed these documents, we know that Barry was involved in bringing the signatures to the event of signing in the first instance, but before implicating him into all of this, I would like Owen to come good first" revealed Graham.

Graham glanced at Gus and said, "Are you right there Gus, you've gone a bit quiet over there"

"No Graham, I am very far from right, I have just brought four thousand head of cattle onto this property and due to bring on another two thousand next month and the only thing that I know about cattle is how to cook and eat them and you are about to arrest the only two guys on this property that knows how to look after six thousand head of cattle," Gus said, "and Graham, I don't mind telling you, that I am fucking worried. Fuck me, I am starting to think the worst thing that happened to me was that fucking phone call from Malcolm. I really don't think that I can handle this anymore, maybe this "curse" is for real".

Graham said, "Sorry old chap, I didn't even consider that, shit yeah, I was too busy with the hunt, you know, wow, this could leave you in a bit of shit".
"It's just me Graham, things tend to get to me a bit, and your guys rubbed me the wrong way today, I felt like hanging one on that prick of a Sergeant, I'll come good" Gus was trying to control his disappointment in things that kept spoiling what they were doing, all the time, it seemed.
Lynette came up to Gus and with her arm around his shoulder said, "I'm on your side darling".

They spoke some more about Owen, Gus suggested that he may not have known what he was signing, maybe he thought he was just witnessing something, which sounded plausible until Lynette asked Gus if he had forgotten that Owen was once a Bank Manager. It was pretty obvious that Sonia had tee'd Owen up to what was happening. Owen would have recognised a Real Estate document surely and not once but twice. It didn't seem that there was anything anyone could say to save Owen. Graham suggested he could let it go for a week or so, but he would have to interview Owen sooner or later, but not much later, and Graham knew he would end up charging Owen on a string of offences that would warrant an arrest.

Ah well, what had to be done, had to be done. Graham would talk to Owen first up tomorrow. But in the interim, beers sounded good and a fairly late night by all was enjoyed by all trying to get poor old Owen off the hook, but to no avail.

They enjoyed a slightly hungover breakfast on the verandah and said their farewells to Graham who would go directly from Owen's place back to Townsville, with Owen as a prisoner, sadly.
Gus headed off to the cattle yards and Lynette was away to Richmond for a few items. Hailee and Janice were cleaning up after breakfast and then onto bed making and house cleaning.

Graham arrived at Owen's and knew instantly that he was not there, even though the Landrover was parked in the shed. Graham knew that Owen had another car that his son Barry had been using while Barry did not have the use of the property's Landcruiser ute, which he now had the use of again. Owen's car was not there, Graham headed towards the cattle yards as he knew they were unloading cattle there this morning. He knew that Owen would not be at the yards, but he could ask Barry where his father had gone, then he thought no, fuck it and turned his car around to head back to Townsville thinking that is a job for the boys in blue.

Neither Gus nor Lynette had spoken about Owen for a couple of days. They were both somewhat moved by the knowledge that Owen would be behind bars in the Townsville watch house. They had become quite fond of Owen.

Barry had not mentioned anything about his dad, he certainly did not appear upset and was right into his work together with Willem as though nothing had happened so neither Lynette or Gus made mention of Owen.

It wasn't until Graham had called Lynette later in the week to tell her that no prints were found on any of the firearms that they had taken from the property including the pistol. The only prints found were on the spent casing and prints on the cartridges in the magazine of the Margolin pistol. Graham, then casually asked if Owen had turned up.

Lynette asked if he had been let out and Graham's answer was that he never got locked up and he explained what had happened that morning he went to interview Owen, so the police now have a lookout for two suspects.

We have found the car that Gus gave to Sonia. The Honda Accord had turned up in Mount Isa where she had sold it privately and the new owner had not yet changed over the registration.

As far as Sonia's location goes, we have not a clue, and Owen's location is also a mystery at this stage. We have his vehicle description and registration numbers out there, but nothing yet.

Graham asked Lynette if there was anything that might have Lachlan's fingerprints lying around the house that she could think of. It would assist in eliminating prints on the cartridges.

Lynette said she would look around but didn't think anything of Lachlan's was in the house which she said, on reflection, why would all the items have disappeared, she had not really had time to consider this point, but why? Graham suggested they may well be there somewhere stowed away.

If I find anything I will call you Lynette promised as she terminated the call. Just then Gus came into the bar to get a beer, "make it two my darling", she called out, "how's the cattle arrivals going".

"A bit slow since Owen's been gone but getting there, Barry is a great worker and young Willem is a fast learner but I think we need another hand and I think I will go and talk to Barry later about finding someone, here cheers", he passed her a stubbie, "I'd better go into town tomorrow to get some more beer and I'll see Peter Lansky and ask him if he knows anyone who might like a job out here, do you want to come with me"."Love to Gus, but the girls and I are setting up a veggie garden tomorrow, but there is a parcel you can collect for me at the Post Office if you would.

"Another" she asked, holding up her stubbie.

Gus took a cold six pack of gold stubbies and drove down to Owen's, which was now Barry's, he supposed. Gus didn't want to upset or get on the wrong side of Barry as now Owen was no longer here, he was relying heavily on him. Both Barry and Willem's Utes were parked in front of the house and they had just arrived and had sat down to enjoy an after work beer. Barry welcomed Gus and said he'd grab a beer, Gus held up the six pack, 'Bush sign language for I've got one here'.

Gus sat down and had a beer with the boys and Barry said that all the cattle were on the property now. Gus said that he would see Lansky tomorrow and ask if he knew of anyone available to work up here. Barry thought that was a good idea, a team of three would be good now that we have about six thousand cattle on board, it would certainly make life a bit easier to look after the three herds of cattle, one at one thousand, three thousand and two thousand, trying to keep them separate is awkward.

Barry also said that we had about six cleanskins in addition to the last count on the last road train. They could have been picked up in error from somewhere but they had no tags so he had them on their own in the old lambing paddock. If nobody claims them then they will be our meat supply. Gus asked how that happens, Barry replied, that the owners didn't do their draft properly or they couldn't be bothered getting them off the truck, it happens.

Willem finished his second beer and said he had better get going as Hailee would be waiting, he said see ya in the morning and started to leave. Barry said "Be here about seven tomorrow and we'll put the big herd up near the top.

After Willem had left Gus said it straight to Barry, "Where's the old fella Barry"
"I'm not sure, I told him not to do anything that Fucking Bitch Sonia was asking him, but she was offering Dad big money just for a bit of help. I think I know where he is, but I am not telling cos I know the coppers will be chasing him"
"I don't want to know his whereabouts, don't even give me a hint so I can't tell anyone, I just hope he is okay, I quite like your dad, I reckon I was getting on well with him."
"He'll be fine Gus, I reckon he will hand himself into the copper's as it's not him really," said Barry and went on to explain that his father refused the money that Sonia had offered him to sign those Real Estate Contracts, and she had offered big dollars, Gus!"

Gus thought that if Owen had not received any money from Sonia then it will go easier on him and he may not even get prison time and expressed his thoughts to Barry, "How well did you get along with Sonia," Gus asked.

Barry shared his thoughts on Sonia to Gus, "I wish she had never come out here, life was pretty good. If mum hadn't gone missing, Sonia would never have been out here".

"I was wondering why your mother wasn't around, but I didn't like to ask Owen"

Barry told Gus that about five years ago his mum's sister in Brisbane, his Auntie Kath, had been ill for some time and it was discovered she had Bowel Cancer. Kath's husband was also getting a bit frail and he was struggling to look after her and it was thought that Auntie Kath did not have very long to live, so Mum had decided to go down to Brisbane and help out as much as she could.

Dad took Mum and two suitcases to the airport in Townsville and said goodbye as she went through the boarding gate and that was the last time we saw her. She never made it to Auntie Kath's house in Ipswich. The taxi she was travelling in was involved in a head on collision on the Warrego Highway about nine kilometres east of Ipswich, mum was sitting in the back of the taxi and was not wearing a seatbelt. It's thought she died instantly and the cab driver didn't even get a scratch.

Ironically, Auntie Kath had died that morning before Mum's plane had even landed at Brisbane airport.

The taxi driver, a Pakistani, was apparently in a hurry to get back to Brisbane to get better fares, apparently the cabbies don't like going out to Ipswich.

It totally destroyed Dad. I don't think Dad would have survived it, had it not been for Lachlan. Dad was suicidal I tell you. Lachlan took Dad for a holiday to the U.S., they must have been gone for over three months. They drove the Route 66, went to Miami, then a short cruise to the Bahamas, back to Miami then drove to Las Vegas in a hired Ford Mustang then flew to New York and then to Scotland, where he showed Dad his old farm at Canonbie. Then they spent some time in London looking around, it was Lachlan's first time in London also, which surprised Dad, what with England being such a small country, that Lachie had not travelled around there before, and when he asked him why it was, he said to dad in his broad Scottish accent, "och laddie, they do na moove aroond here mooch, thee may as well be a fooking tree, laddie:.

Even when they got back they didn't stay for long, they went down to Sydney and stayed at the Star Casino and visited Darling Harbour and all the attractions, then from there to Melbourne, then Perth and then finally back home.

Barry said that 'Bitch' Sonia was fuming. She was telling people that she had not felt well and that is why Owen went away with Lachlan rather than her.

But Dad and Lachie returned and went away again, that is when, according to Barry, Sonia started the rumour that Lachlan and my father were gay.

"I tell you, that "Fucking Bitch Sonia" is a real piece of work" Barry concluded.

Owen Harrigan

Lynette had left her mobile on the counter of the bar at the house, when Gus had walked in to get a drink after returning from Richmond, the phone was ringing away with Lynette's obscure music theme that was known to no- one.

"Lynette's phone" he answered, wishing he had grabbed a beer before answering.
"Gus, Graham here, how's it all going mate!"
"Mate, it's all good, got all the cattle on, I just got back from town with some more grog, employed another guy to start tomorrow, just about to have a beer and…that's about me".

Graham said, "Well I do have some news, well actually quite a bit of news, and I do need to get a couple of pics from your place that the boffins took but seemed to have erased themselves.
Would you guys mind having a guest, two actually, Stefanie said she would love to come out too, but she doesn't think we should push ourselves upon you and wants to stay at the pub in Richmond"

"Bullshit!, you'll be staying here, in fact, Barry had the Mobile Butcher out here and we have some nice beef just setting and should be ready tomorrow, Lynette'll be over the moon, she loves visitors out here" Gus answered. And Graham added that they should be here at about four pm.

Gus went out to his ute to continue putting the slabs of beer into the cool room, and a carton, just as well, of Oyster Bay Sauvignon Blanc. He then got the two, fairly heavy boxes that he collected from the post office addressed to Lynette and placed them in the entry.

Gus then went back into the bar and found Lynette in there, she had gone into the bar as she thought she heard her telephone ringing. Gus had told her that he had taken the call and also the news that they were having visitors tomorrow afternoon and he gave her the details.

"I just wish all this shit would end," said Lynette, "don't get me wrong, I am looking forward to seeing Stefanie and of course Graham, but I really have had enough of all the drama we seem to be having, or had around here, I just want things to go nicely the way it is just now, with the cattle, the house is looking perfect, we are into the veggie garden, then we are going to start fixing up the Manager's House for Janice, Hailee and Willem. It's all just going really nice and I just want all of this other business gone, no more. Let's just all get on with life and forget the past on the place and turn this place into a dream".

Gus agreed, he'd had a gut full of whatever had happened here, and did not need to think about it. He was interested now in the cattle that he had to look after for the next six months and then he had to find replacement agistments for the property. He did not need any more drama, it was spoiling his new environment. He also agreed that they should forget all the sad past history and get on with life.

"Cheer's," said Lynette, holding up her stubbie.
"Double Cheer's," said Gus, holding up two fresh stubbies from the bar fridge.

The next day was just perfect, as it was this time of year, just a tad hot today at 38°c but cool overnight at 19°c and no rain on the horizon until at least late December. But all is good.

Gus went over to the meat room at the cattle yards, which was just a large mobile cool room that had its four wheels removed and sat on blocks. It was connected to the power that ran to the cattle yards to power the water pumps and various equipment that was used there.
Inside the meat room, the temp was about 12°c and was an instant relief when Gus walked in. The room was two point four metres by six metres and had three stainless steel benches, a band saw and a tool rack with bone cutters and hand saws, knives were placed in scabbards attached to the benches. A large stainless steel wash tub with hot and cold water taps was incorporated into another small bench and another standard type of double kitchen sink. At the end of the meat room next to the cool air outlet were two long rails for hooks to hang on, running the two point four metre length.

Hanging from the rails was a full half of hindquarter beef, a full half of forequarter beef and another half of beef separated into various whole cuts. Gus took one of two midsections and with the bandsaw cut four tomahawk steaks of about five hundred grams each.

Graham and Stefanie arrived at around four o clock as he said he would and both Lynette and Gus greeted them at the porte-cochere, and after all the air kisses and hugs and hello's led them to the cool verandah and procured drinks for all. Graham excused himself and asked if he could take the couple of photos that forensics required and then he could relax, "go for it" Lynette said. "Where is it that you need to photograph", asked Gus. Graham explained it was three angles of the ceiling framing where the access door was located. That out of the way Graham said, "Let me fill you in on the latest in the saga of" Woolgar River Park", but before he could continue, Lynette cut in.

"Graham, don't take offence, but we have had a gut full of the so called saga and have just about lost interest. We think it causing a great disruption to our lives to the extent that it may be detrimental to our continuing to live here and we have decided to forget all about the past issues with respect to this place, the bottom line is, just get on with a new chapter in our lives," said Lynette.

The area around them on the verandah went silent for a moment and Stefanie did not know where to look, she was always telling Graham not to bring his work home with him as it truly did give her the shit's hearing about police matters day in and day, out and now he was destroying a friendship through his police talk. Lynette went to get a round of drinks.

Lynette got back with the drinks and Graham, not put off in the slightest, as thick as two short planks, Lynette thought, continued by saying, "Well that's good, because what I have to tell you will bring to a conclusion all the events at this property," then after a long pause while he took a drink and sat back in his chair, "that is, of course, if you would like to hear it".

Graham produced his laptop from its bag and proceeded to read to them all a 'Confidential' Police Report from Victoria in relation to charges pending against Richard Kemp.

The report basically said he was a Solicitor with an office in Horsham and that he specialised in Property Conveyancing. Apparently Kemp was a bit of a failure due to his laziness and drinking, and gambling problems. Conveyancing, however, was a reasonably simple task that needed very little input from him and he employed two female clerks who had good previous Conveyancing experience from law firms in Melbourne but were looking for an escape to the country.

Kemp, it seemed was very rarely in the office anytime after eleven in the mornings. He could be found at any local race meetings in the district or at the Horsham Sporties Club.

His business in Firebrace Street was quite buoyant and he was known to extend his services to help his mates out of difficult situations at times, not always exactly legal.

When Jason Strange presented an opportunity to Kemp, that could result in a very substantial margin of around the two million dollar mark, then Richard Kemp was all for it.

The first thing that popped up when doing a property search, the female clerk noticed a discrepancy in the sale price of the property to approximate valuations. Secondly, that the buyer was a company that had been registered in Victoria very recently. One of the Directors was named Susan Little, whom the clerk knew to be Richard Kemp's wife, as Little was her maiden name. Thirdly there was no legal proof of the seller's identities, which is required by law. The settlement funds were to be paid into a bank account in the name of Sonia Teague, not a combined account of the vendors.

But there also seemed to be a conflict of interest as Kemp Solicitors appeared to be acting on behalf of the buyer and the seller.

When the clerk advised Richard Kemp of these peculiarities, he just shrugged them off and told the clerk that nothing was untoward other than the conflict but he could fix that by using his name. Richard Kemp on one client and the Company name, Kemp Solicitors on the other and everything would be above board. The conveyancing clerk was doubtful, but Kemp was the legal eagle so...

In a nutshell, Strange and Kemp had registered C company called Qld Associated Pastoral Pty Ltd with two directors being each of their wives using their maiden names, perfectly legal.

The Company signed an offer to purchased the property "Woolgar River Park" for two point one million dollars and paid a deposit of ten per cent, two hundred and ten thousand dollars, to the Real Estate agent Jason Strange. This deposit, although receipted, does not appear to have been paid into any bank account related to the Real Estate office in Charters Towers.

This Company's property purchase intended to retain the property for a short period of time, say two years or more and show consecutive financial operational losses, then dispose of the property at a market valuation of around seven million dollars. The Company would then go into liquidation and avoid capital gains tax of around nine hundred thousand dollars and each Director would end up with three point five million dollars each for their original outlay of one million and five thousand dollars. A profit each of two million, four hundred and ninety five thousand dollars, not a bad two year profit.

Graham put away his laptop and finished his drink. "Wow", said Lynette and Gus agreed, and said that contrary to what they had said to Graham earlier, that was interesting.

Graham cut in and said, "The best is yet to come, let me get drinks this time, I have a load of them in the boot which will be getting hotter." Gus helped Graham put the drinks into the cool room, then took cold ones to place into the refrigerator at the bar.

"Well", Graham commenced, "Owen Harrigan walked into the Townsville police station yesterday morning and handed himself in and later that morning was charged with the murder of Lachlan Teague".

Graham took delight in looking at the three astonished faces. He took a long drink and then commenced. Graham told them that when he entered the police station he asked at the reception desk to see me. I had actually only just arrived there when the Desk Sergeant called me and told me who wanted to see me and should he be escorted up to my office, to which I agreed.

Owen entered my office door and greeted me like an old friend and said that he believed I was looking for him. I corrected him and said the police were looking for him to which he replied that they couldn't be looking too hard as he had been waiting in reception to see me for the last ten minutes.

We both laughed together then Owen said to me in a very serious voice that he needs to talk to me about something, and I asked if was it about the Real Estate Contract signatures, as that has nothing to do with me but I will get the Fraud Squad Officer to talk to him if he wished.

Owen said it had nothing to do with the real estate contracts but about Lachlan Teague.
He said that he had not seen Lachlan for a while and Sonia kept fending him off saying he was asleep or in the shower or too ill to talk. Anyway, he got fed up with being fobbed off and messed around and decided to get physical with her and force his way in past her, but he didn't really want to hurt her because if Owen was as sick as she says he is, then she is caring for him and if she got the shits too much she might piss off and then there was no one to care for Lachie.

Anyway, he was determined to see Lachie and he approached the house and rattled on the door very loudly. She would normally shout out "Yes, yes, what do you want, who is it", but this day no sound. He could not tell if she was out as the garages were always shut and locked, the place was like a fort. But Owen had seen her retrieve a key from a large concrete bowl near the laundry door and this day he went to look for it. It was easily found and he opened the laundry door and replaced the key. He found Lachie upstairs in his bed and the very sight of him made Owen gasp, the man was a wreck, a complete and utter wreck. He was awake and he looked at me in recognition and as I approached him he muttered "pain". Owen wasn't sure what he said and Lachie repeated the word "pain" and then Lachie said feebly "Get ma gun from the wee desk and shoot me, ah canna handle this no more, you must get ma gun noo ah tell yer".

Owen told him no way would I get his gun for him, and he begged me, he was crying and he begged me. Owen with a very pained voice continued to say that he went to the desk, he knew where it was as they had taken it out shooting from time to time. He removed the polished timber case from the drawer and placed it on the desktop, opened each clasp and took the pistol from the case. He picked up the magazine that was kept loaded and slid it into the receiver inside the handle and then holding the pistol in his right hand and placing his left forefinger and middle finger on the cocking grips fixed to the action slide, he pulled it back and the pistol was loaded and ready.

He took the pistol over to Lachlan and in tears, handed it to him, Lachlan with great effort, took hold of the pistol in his left hand, placed the barrel awkwardly in his left ear and without any hesitation, he pulled the trigger.

Owen told Graham, that he could not believe what had just happened. He couldn't believe he had handed the gun to

Lachlan as he was ordered to do so, as he knew it was wrong but he also knew that the man was in great pain and agony. He could not believe that Lachlan had placed the gun into his ear, so quickly that he doubted that he could have taken it from him before he pulled the trigger. He said there was little noise as the pistol discharged, the sound was more like when you pop the top from a stubbie, just a FSSST sound and that was it, Lachlan was dead.

The recoil from the Margolin had shaken the pistol loose from Lachlan's hand and the pistol clattered to the floor. Owen looked at Lachlan, his eyes now looked peaceful and his face no longer contorted, there was no sign of blood, even when Owen looked into Lachlan's ear there was no sign of blood. Owen lifted Lachlan's head where he knew there would be the exit hole and blood, but there was none. Owen placed Lachlan's head back onto his pillow and retrieved the pistol, took it into the bathroom and with a towel carefully wiped it clean, removed the magazine and also wiped it clean, then carrying the pistol and the magazine in the towel he placed them back into their case, closed the case and carefully wiped it.

Owen was about to replace the pistol in the desk drawer but he had a thought, he remembered the secret compartment that Curtis had made when building the house and he thought to place the Margolin in there so that Sonia could not find it and then he remembered Lachlan's rifle and his shotgun and thought it may be a good idea to place them in there also, for what real reason he didn't know. He then left the house and waited for Sonia's call, which came the following morning.

Graham got up and again got the drinks as the others were too astonished to even move.

"What will happen to him now" asked Gus.

"I went with him down to Homicide and told the Sergeant there to take his statement, charge him murder but to look after him" Graham said, "the most likely scenario would be Manslaughter and I think that under the circumstances and with a good Lawyer, then he probably won't even do gaol time. With the other matter in respect to the Real Estate contracts, he received no profit and he signed his own name, he didn't try to forge Lachlan's name, the real crook there is Sonia.

"What's the word on Sonia" asked Lynette.

"We found out that her real name is Sonia Herin, she's an Italian. She comes from a town called Villaciambra which is near Palermo in the south of Italy, and that's where we found her. When we were first looking for her it involved possible murder charges where we can obtain extradition, but now with the charges relating only to fraud and bits and pieces, it's probably not worth the effort.

If she should ever return to Australia we will pick her up the moment she lands here.

"I am so glad you came here tonight" Gus said as he was getting more drinks, "I am sure that both Lynette and I will sleep much better".

Graham summed it all up saying the whole saga has been quite incredible.
It starts with Sonia selling the property, she doesn't own through a shonky Real Estate Agent who himself with a shonky Solicitor sets up a Company to purchase the property for far less than it's value.
The shonky Solicitor pushes through the Conveyancing without establishing the legal ownership of the vendors of the property. Approving the settlement funds to be paid into a bank account with a solitary name that is alien to the property title.

All approved but, within seven days of settlement, a new owner pops up! All because of Lachlan making a will with Malcolm and Malcolm becoming aware of Lachlan's death and contacting Angus.

Otherwise, the settlement would have been finalised, the money deposited into Sonia's account and she would be back to Italy, a rich lady. Nobody would have been the wiser.

And then of course, had anyone other than Lynette found the spent twenty two casing, it would most likely have been discarded to the rubbish bin and there would have been nothing suspect about Lachlan's death.

The 'curse' that the Aboriginal, Kurrie is said to have placed on the property. Was it responsible for the demise of the Southwell family or just tragic consequences, the death of Owen's wife Jenny?

The death of Lachlan, who knows?

But did you know that there was a massacre on, or near this property in 1881 following the murder of a police sub inspector named Henry Kaye, by an Aboriginal he had taken prisoner with a group of others? It is rumoured that Inspector Kaye's men were deeply distressed at his death and massacred the entire group.

One can read into things, whatever one wants, who knows. History such as we know about this property would scare some away, others would shrug their shoulders and just get on and enjoy life.

Anyway, it's your shout.

www.ingramcontent.com/pod-product-compliance
Lightning Source LLC
Chambersburg PA
CBHW071925290426
44110CB00013B/1486